Published by
ATLANTIC
PUBLISHERS & DISTRIBUTORS (P) LTD
7/22, Ansari Road, Darya Ganj,
New Delhi-110002
Phones : +91-11-40775252, 23273880, 23275880, 23280451
Fax : +91-11-23285873
Web : www.atlanticbooks.com
E-mail : orders@atlanticbooks.com

Branch Office
5, Nallathambi Street, Wallajah Road,
Chennai-600002
Phones : +91-44-64611085, 32413319
E-mail : chennai@atlanticbooks.com

ISBN 978-81-269-1392-3

Printed in India at Nice Printing Press, A-33/3A, Site-IV, Industrial Area, Sahibabad, Ghaziabad, U.P.

To my mother for her selflessness
and the courage with which she
struggled against all odds

Preface

Based on a decade-long fieldwork in the city of Kolkata, I have tried to describe the child labour problem in a Third World urban situation in this book. This book is a part of my continuous effort to develop a Third Worldly understanding of marginalisation of population in general and child labour problem in particular. The problem of child labour has been explored in the Third World city of Kolkata in the backdrop of globalisation and its attendant marginalisation of population in the urban areas of the Third World. This form of urban marginalisation, which has been further exacerbated with the advent of globalisation, is primarily the result of the state's failure to provide adequate basic services to the city dwellers. I found from my study that with the gradual withdrawal of the state from various spheres of life of its citizens, particularly the vulnerable sections of the population, under the conditionalities of WTO regime neither the problem of marginalisation nor the problem of child labour will be reduced in the foreseeable future.

I explored this approach by conducting decade-long fieldwork in the city of Kolkata where I studied three different settlements (Population-I, Population-II and Population-III). Population-I and Population-II were 'illegal' squatter settlements where the inhabitants were living without any security of tenure on the land of their settlements. I also found that the people in these two settlements were living without the basic services required for living. Both of these settlements were eroded from the landscape of the city during the course of this fieldwork to undertake some city development programme and the people living in these two settlements were evicted. Population-III, on the other hand, was a recognised slum where the people were living with some kind of security of tenure under an act called Calcutta Thika and Other Tenancies and Lands (Acquisition and Regulation) Act, 1981. I considered Population-III as the Programme Group since it has got a programme in the form of security of tenure and Population-I and Population-II, in a combined way, as the Control Group. I found substantial differences in the standard of living as well as other aspects of life between these two groups because of the security of tenure programme. It was found that the incidents of child labour came to a negligible level in the Programme Group as they felt more protected after having earned security of tenure of their living space. Control Group, on the other hand, was the hotbed of child labour as the parents in the Control Group used to expose their children to the ruthless labour market at a very early age. One of the reasons for this prevalence of child labour in the Control Group was the insecurity among the inhabitants of Population-I and Population-II regarding their living space.

In the first two chapters I have introduced the work as well as incorporated a discussion on the concepts of child labour as well as the magnitude of child labour in Third World. In the third chapter I have briefly discussed the research design of this work in the first section. In the next nine sections of this chapter I have elucidated in detail the findings of my decade-long fieldwork where I took up various aspects of the population like the profile of the populations, educational aspects of the population, integration with the urban life, economic aspects of the population, population and educational profiles of the child labourers, economic profile of the child labourers, thick description of the key behaviours and statistical analyses of the marginalisation of population and child labour. In the last chapter I have summarized my observations and developed ideas on how a Third Worldly understanding on this problem can emerge which is essential for properly comprehending the problem of child labour, a predominantly Third World occurrence.

I am immensely grateful to Dr. Sudhendu Mukherjee and Dr. Syamalkanti Sengupta for their guidance and cooperation during this work. I am also indebted to Arnab Das and Siddhartha Dasgupta for commenting on various parts of this book. During a crucial stage of my work I got immense help from Dr. Suranjan Sengupta and Dr. Debapriya Sengupta who gave invaluable suggestions as well as inputs on the statistical aspects of this work. I would also like to thank Dipak Shome for typing a part of this work and Kallol Dasgupta for taking pictures of the field. I also feel indebted to Dr. Nibedita Chakrabarti, Priyadarsini Sengupta, Soma Ray Chaudhuri and Subrata Basak for their valuable contributions at the different stages of this work.

The book will be useful to the students, teachers and researchers of socio-economics, policymakers and administrators. The common readers will find it informative.

Subrata Sankar Bagchi

Contents

Preface .... *v*

List of Tables .... *xi*

List of Plates .... *xvi*

1. Introduction 1-4

2. Child Labour in the Third World 5-31
   - Determinants of Child Labour 5
   - Magnitude of the Problem of Child Labour 7
   - Major Child Labour-Intensive Occupations in India 9
   - Official Reports on Child Labour in India ... 10
   - Constitutional Safeguards on Child Labour in India 13
   - Legal Provisions on Child Labour in India ... 14
   - Other National Initiatives on Child Labour in India 19
   - International Initiatives on Child Labour 21

3. Design, Results and Analyses 32-129
   - Section I: Outlining the Research Design...... 32
   - Section II: Profile of the Populations 38
   - Section III: Educational Aspects of the Populations 42
   - Section IV: Condition of Urban Marginality among the Studied Population 46
   - Section V: Economic Condition of the

Populations 51

Section VI: Population and Educational Profiles of the Child Labourers 60

Section VII: Economic Profile of the Child Labourers 64

Section VIII: Thick Description of the Key Behaviours 80

Section IX: Statistical Analyses on the Marginalisation of Population and Child Labour 91

Section X: Tables 102

4. Child Labour in a Third World Urban Situation: Towards a Conclusion 130-146

Child Labour in the Third World 131

The Research Design and the Findings 132

Towards a Third Worldly Discourse 145

Bibliography 147-153

Appendix: Plates 154-158

Index 159-160

List of Tables

Table 3.9.1: The Aspects to be Observed on Urban Marginalisation 92

Table 3.9.2: Housing Condition and Some Collective Consumption Facilities in the Control Group 94

Table 3.9.3: Housing Condition and Some Collective Consumption Facilities in the Programme Group 95

Table 3.10.1: Distribution of the Populations According to Age and Sex 102

Table 3.10.2: Distribution of the Populations According to Child-Woman Ratio (0-4 Years) 103

Table 3.10.3: Distribution of the Populations According to Child-Woman Ratio (5-9 Years) 103

Table 3.10.4: Distribution of the Populations According to Child-Woman Ratios 103

Table 3.10.5: Distribution of the Populations According to the Standard of Education 104

Table 3.10.6: Distribution of the Populations According to the Overall Literacy 105

Table 3.10.7: Distribution of the Populations According to the Child Literacy 106

Table 3.10.8: Distribution of the Populations According to the Place of Birth 107

Table 3.10.9: Distribution of the Populations According to the Holding of Ration Card 107

Table 3.10.10: Distribution of the Populations According to the Voting Status 107

Table 3.10.11: Distribution of the Households According to the Presence of Some Indicators on Collective Consumption .. 108

Table 3.10.12: Distribution of the Populations According to the Persons in Labour Force and Persons Actually Working..... 109

Table 3.10.13: Distribution of the Populations According to the Incidence of Unemployment 109

Table 3.10.14: Distribution of the Populations According to the Children in Labour Force and Children Actually Working... 110

Table 3.10.15: Distribution of the Working Population According to the Working Children and Working Adults 110

Table 3.10.16: Distribution of the Working Population According to the Types of Primary Occupation 111

Table 3.10.17: Distribution of the Households According to the Family Income Per Day 112

Table 3.10.18: Distribution of the Households According to the Level of Monthly Savings 112

Table 3.10.19: Distribution of the Child Labourers According to Age and Sex 113

Table 3.10.20:	Distribution of the Child Labourers and the Children Populations According to Age and Sex	113
Table 3.10.21:	Distribution of the Child Labourers According to the Standard of Education	114
Table 3.10.22:	Distribution of the Child Labourers According to the Years of Schooling	114
Table 3.10.23:	Distribution of the Literate Child Labourers According to the Continuity of Study	115
Table 3.10.24:	Distribution of the Child Labourers According to the Main Reason for Leaving/Not Sending to School	115
Table 3.10.25:	Distribution of the Child Labourers According to the Status as Labourer	116
Table 3.10.26:	Distribution of the Child Labourers According to the Age of Entering Work	116
Table 3.10.27:	Distribution of the Child Labourers According to the Working Hours Per Day	117
Table 3.10.28:	Distribution of the Child Labourers According to the Availability of Resting Time within the Working Hours	117
Table 3.10.29:	Distribution of the Child Labourers According to the Number of Working Days in a Week	118
Table 3.10.30:	Distribution of the Child Labourers According to the Type of Sector of the Economy They Work	118
Table 3.10.31:	Distribution of the Child Labourers According to the Type of Primary Occupation	119

Table 3.10.32: Distribution of the Child Labourers According to the Primary Occupation (Details of Occupations) 120

Table 3.10.33: Distribution of the Child Labourers According to the Nature of Work 121

Table 3.10.34: Distribution of the Child Labourers According to the Level of Daily Income 121

Table 3.10.35: Distribution of the Child Labourers According to the Distance of the Workplace 122

Table 3.10.36: Distribution of the Child Labourers According to the Mode of Transport to the Workplace 122

Table 3.10.37: Distribution of the Child Labourers According to the Part of Earning Spent on Transport to the Workplace 123

Table 3.10.38: Distribution of the Child Labourers According to the Time Spent to Travel to the Workplace 123

Table 3.10.39: Distribution of the Child Labourers According to the Facilities Available at the Workplaces 124

Table 3.10.40: Distribution of the Child Labourers According to the Number of Accidents. Happened in Working Life 125

Table 3.10.41: Distribution of Wage-Earning Child Labourers According to the Number of Employees Present in the Working Unit 125

Table 3.10.42: Distribution of Wage-Earning Child Labourers According to the Recipients of the Wage 126

Table 3.10.43: Distribution of Wage-Earning Child Labourers According to the Type of the Fellow Employees' Behaviour in the Workplace 126

Table 3.10.44: Distribution of the Wage-Earning Child Labourers According to the Type of Employer's Behaviour in the Workplace 127

Table 3.10.45: Distribution of the Child Labourers According to the Mode of Receiving Wage or Income 127

Table 3.10.46: Distribution of the Child Labourers According to the Presence or Absence of Family 128

Table 3.10.47: Distribution of the Child Labourers According to the Contribution of His/Her Income to the Household......... 128

Table 3.10.48: Distribution of the Child Labourers According to the Level of Dependence of the Household on His/Her Income ... 128

Table 3.10.49: Distribution of the Child Labourers According to the Level of His/Her Own Spending from His/Her Earning ... 129

Table 3.10.50: Distribution of the Child Labourers According to the Frequency of Leaving Job 129

Table 3.10.51: Distribution of the Child Labourers According to the Reason for Leaving Job 129

List of Plates

Plate A1: The Picture from the Field (The Settlement) 154

Plate A2: The Picture from the Field (The Settlement Beside the Railway Tract) 155

Plate A3: The Picture from the Field (The Waste/Rag Pickers) 156

Plate A4: The Picture from the Field (A Family of Child Labourers) 157

Plate A5: The Picture from the Field (Children Working in a Small Workshop) 158

1

Introduction

There are plenty of scholarly monographs on child labour available in the ever expanding printing market each bringing its own view on this problem but very few of them had analysed the effect of globalisation and marginalisation on the phenomenon of child labour and even fewer actually tried find out a Third Worldly understanding of the problem. This has become an urgent imperative now as the phenomenon of child labour is predominantly a Third World reality though the author does deny the presence of child labour in developed world. This book, which is an outcome of a study spanning over a decade on the problem of child labour in association with the problem of marginalisation of population in Kolkata, has tried to analyse the child labour problem in the backdrop of liberalisation of economy of India and also endeavoured to bring out a Third Worldly understanding of the problem. This research was started during the early years of 1990s when India as a nation jumped into the bandwagon of GATT/WTO regime immediately after a crippling balance of payment crisis. Some observers during that time warned the government of a serious predicament from the experiences from several Latin American and African countries where the GATT regime had imposed strict Structural Adjustment Programmes (SAP) from 1980s. Due to the SAP-related measures those countries were facing increased inequality, deprivation, loss of livelihood, evictions, alienation and violence which led to increase marginalisation of a huge number of people in these countries. Cities in these countries became more affected as with transnational form of economy cities became the centre of attraction for the footloose capital which forced the local governments to take up various city beautification-cum-development programmes even at the cost of evicting the poor and vulnerable section of population. To make the things worse these Third World cities became the destination of teeming millions from the rural areas as they have lost their subsistence due to the strict SAP-related measure leading to the suffering of even larger part of humanity.

With this background in mind the author started this study on the problem of child labour in association with the problem of urban marginalisation in the Third World city of Kolkata under the SAP regime. The phenomenon of urban marginalisation has been defined here as the inability of the market economy or the state policies to provide adequate shelter and urban basic services (explained here as collective consumption in line with Castells 1977, 1983) to an increasing proportion of urban population. Urban marginalisation is viewed here as the result of a struggle over the urban space among the different sections of the population. This study will also show how this struggle has intensified with the advent of globalisation and the implementation of several SAP-induced measures in the city. Thus with the progress of globalisation local authorities were forced to introduce various measures like the creation of new infrastructures for the legitimate city-dwellers and/or users of the urban facilities causing the eviction of several illegal as well as legitimised settlements in the city. These acts of settlements, on the one hand, did change the city landscape and served the legal users of the basic services much better. On the other hand, it caused losing of survival network of protection to the vulnerable section of the urban population and in most cases drove these people to even worsened living conditions than they were living before the eviction (Bagchi 2004, 2005).

During this study the fieldwork was concentrated on three different settlements in the city of Kolkata and a long-term, intensive ethnographic fieldwork among the people of those settlements had been conducted. These three different groups of population were primarily selected on the basis of their differential condition of urban marginality in the city of Kolkata. Population-I and Population-II were the illegal squatter settlements and Population-III was a recognised slum settlement in the city of

Kolkata. Dwellers of the first two settlements did not have any security of tenure and during the course of this study and they were evicted from both the settlements. Population-I was evicted for widening the existing flyover in the Park Circus region of Kolkata and Population-II for the implementation of Ganga Action Plan under which the Beliaghata Canal (Population-II was on the side to this canal) was to be dredged and made navigable. Both the measures were taken as part of the city beautification/development programmes which was essential for the local authority to attract new investment in the city as well as in the province of West Bengal. Population-III, on the other hand, was a recognised slum where the residents were living with a kind of security of tenure as they had received *pattas* (entitlement) from the government under the provision of Calcutta *Thika* Tenancy Act, 1981 and got the right of *Thika* Tenants from the government—a right that ensured one to live on the land and build a house but the owner could not sell the land. Thus Population-I as well as Population-II, in a combined way, were considered here as the Control Group with no programme of security of tenure. Population-III was observed as the Programme Group with its residents enjoyed some programme in the form of security of tenure due to *Thika* Tenancy Act for over two decades before the start of this work.

Findings of this fieldwork suggested that poverty and marginalisation in a Third World city like Kolkata became an integral part of the neo-liberal model of globalisation and this form of globalisation widened the social and economic disparity existing within the society. It also dragged new groups of people into poverty and displaced many marginalised people from their settlements which caused in the breakdown of their existing support systems. This study showed that with the advent of globalisation people living without any security of tenure of their settlements became more vulnerable and some of these settlements were demolished to built roads or for other purposes as part of city beautification/development projects. These marginalised people joined in the ill-paid, irregular sector of economy in huge numbers and they were also releasing their children to the workforce at a very tender age as part of their survival strategy. They did not consider education as an essential criterion for their children since they could not see their future beyond the next day and investing in the education of their children (or letting their children to study instead of work which was a sacrifice for these people) considered a 'deferred investment' which these people could not afford. This had a spiralling effect as the working children could not earn enough for their families and the families remained in perpetual poverty and vulnerability. At the same time the future of these families along with the entire population remained similarly uncertain with their future force working from the tender age. These children went through immense physical, cognitive, emotional and moral hazards from a very early age and were deprived of their childhood to support their families. But the question remained whether it would be justified to take away childhood from these children in the name of supporting their families and whether childhood would remain the right of privileged few? What the government could and should do in this regard to end or minimise this form of deprivation? How could the government be made sensible to act against this deprivation? It looks like a vicious cycle and the author will examine this cycle in some detail in this monograph.

2

Child Labour in the Third World

DETERMINANTS OF CHILD LABOUR

Studies on child labour stressed on culturally-relative definition(s) of child labour that has not yet emerged but one can certainly agree on a generic characterisations of this child labour that it is the "work which impairs the health and development of children" (Fyfe 1989: 4) and "a denial of the right to education and of the opportunity to reach full physical and psychological development" (ILO 1996: 8). In most of these characterisations child labourers have been referred to the children under 14 years old who work in both the formal and informal sectors, in conditions that are harmful or potentially harmful to the children. Observers also included underpayment of children for their work, which is a common occurrence, and other forms of exploitation. According to some observers education forms the fundamental human right for every child and any child below the age of 14 years who is out of school must be treated as a working child. Thus over 100 million out-of-school children between 5 and 14 years should be regarded as working children. They also hold that it is the primary duty of the state to provide education to its citizens and to universalise education which will prevent its children to slip into workforce at a tender age. Other observers believe that considering the magnitude of the problem, child labour cannot be eradicated overnight and a gradual approach of withdrawing children from hazardous work coupled with the rehabilitation of the children working in non-hazardous work. Still others believe that it should be left to the children to decide whether or not they want to go to the school and if due to the dull as well as irrelevant educational system deter children from school they should be let free to work.

In the absence of any consensus on this issue the author found it imperative to observe the matter at the household level where the households decide regarding how children's time will be allocated between leisure, schooling, household activities and employment. This anthropological study conducted a long-term fieldwork among some marginalised families to observe which factor influences the households to decide that their children would be involved released for work. He found that the absence of security of tenure had resulted frequent evictions of their settlements making them more vulnerable. This vulnerability influenced the households to release their children for work at a very tender age and the households, in front of the lurking danger of getting evicted. These household could not decide positively on the education of their children. But one should not consider the household factors in isolation and should contextualise it with other factors which are external to the households schooling environment, the demand for child labour in that society, the legal aspects of phenomenon and the cultural context of child labour in the society under study. One should also consider the effect of globalisation on this phenomenon as with the advent of globalised market states stopped to act as a buffer for the vulnerable section of the population leaving them on their own to fight against the ruthless market forces which responds only to the needs of the riches. The ultimate determinants of child labour are a complex interaction among various factors acting at different levels which might be different in different society. Since child labour is predominantly a Third World phenomenon one should have more specific studies on child labour situation in these countries so that a Third Worldly understanding of this problem can emerge.

The author, when faced with the specifics of child labour problem in India found that the welfare of children in general and the problem of child labour in particular are the areas of great concern and serious questions can be raised on the faith and commitment of successive governments in India in this regard. Let us start by exploring how big is the problem of child labour in India in comparison with some other countries in the world.

MAGNITUDE OF THE PROBLEM OF CHILD LABOUR

According to the 1971 Census, the estimated figure of working children was 10.7 million, which increased to 13.6 million as per the 1981 Census but declined to 11.28 million as per 1991 Census. According to the data of Central Labour Ministry of Government of India the number was 15.6 million in 1989-90 and 17.0 million in 1992-93. The same report views that in every year the increase is about .5 million. Operation Research Group Survey of 1983-84 indicates that there are 44 million child labourers in India. Census 2001 put the figure of child labour to 12.7 million. But according to some unofficial estimation this number is now as high as 40 million to 110 million now.

According to census data the number of working children has somewhat fallen both in absolute and percentage terms during the period between 1981 and 1991. In 1981, child labour population was 2 per cent of the total population while in 1991 this population works out to 1.34 per cent. The number of working children as a percentage of the child population has also fallen from 7.6 per cent in 1981 to 5.2 per cent in 1991. Similar fall in percentages of child labour in comparison to the workforce was perceptible as in 1981 6 per cent of the workforce was child labourer while 1991 this percentage was 3.59 per cent. But 2001 Census data showed an increase in child labour in absolute terms from 11.28 million to 12.7 million though there was slight decline in percentage terms. The proportion of working children to the total labour force (5.2 per cent) is also lower in India than in some other developing countries like Turkey (27.3 per cent), Thailand (20.7 per cent), Bangladesh (19.5 per cent), Brazil (18.8 per cent), Pakistan (16.6 per cent), Indonesia (12.4 per cent), Mexico (11.5 per cent), Egypt (8.2 per cent) or Argentina (6.6 per cent). This picture of declining child labour population would hardly reflect the true picture as the absolute number according to official census data continues to be exceedingly high, and in fact is the highest in world.

Again, the official figures cannot also be taken as final as ILO has recently criticised India for its effort to hide the truth about the country's child labourers (Majumdar 2001). In a recent ILO meeting (2001) in Phuket, Thailand, the Indian Ministry of Labour tried to counter the claims by the human rights bodies and other NGOs that millions of Indian children were engaged in the worst forms of child labour and termed the estimates 'range from pure guesswork to over-generation from small samples'. But ILO censured the Indian Government report as sketchy and unrealistic (cited in Majumdar 2001).

The province with the highest child labour population in the country is Uttar Pradesh which as per 2001 Census had 1.92 million working children. Other States where child labour populations are more than one million are Andhra Pradesh (1.36 million), Rajasthan (1.26 million), Bihar (1.11 million) and Madhya Pradesh (1.06 million). The state of West Bengal stands little lower in this list with little over 4 per cent (0.85 million in absolute terms) child labourer population. The distribution of child labour in different states appears to indicate certain co-relations. The trend suggests that the states with a larger population living below the poverty line have a higher incidence of child labour. A higher incidence of child labour is also accompanied by a high drop-out rate in schools.

Child labour in India is still more of a rural than an urban phenomenon as more than 90 per cent child labour is engaged in rural areas, agriculture and allied employments like cultivation, agricultural labour, livestock, forestry and fisheries. In urban areas, manufacturing, service and repair accounts for about 8.64 per cent of child labour and only about 0.8 per cent work in factories. The unorganised as well as informal sector of economy accounts for almost the entire child labour force, both in urban and rural areas.

Another fact very much worthwhile to mention here that the overwhelming majority of child labourers in India come from the communities and groups which are at the lower rungs of our traditional, caste-based social hierarchy, i.e. the Scheduled Castes (SC), Scheduled Tribes (ST), Other Backward Classes (OBC) and minorities, especially the Muslims. These also constitute the bulk of the small and marginal peasantry, landless and agricultural labourers and artisan groups. This amounts to the majority of the Indian population. These, in short are the poor of India and it is from the families and communities of the poor that the child labourers come. It is therefore, not accidental that studies of many of the industries where there is a substantial presence of child labour like the carpet industry, the match, brass-ware, glass and bangle, lock-making, slate, gem-polishing industries and the tea plantations show that the overwhelming majority of the children working in these industries come from Scheduled Castes, Scheduled Tribes, Other Backward Classes and Muslim communities. Thus the communities which supply the bulk of India's child labourers are the victims of a social system which is characterised by unequal access to the principal productive resources and assets.

MAJOR CHILD LABOUR-INTENSIVE OCCUPATIONS IN INDIA

In India there are many occupations where child labourers are employed in high numbers. Major child labour-intensive occupations in India are as follows (for an earlier overall account see Dingwaney 1988):

(i) *Match and Fire Works* in Sivakasi (Tamil Nadu) employing 50,000 to 80,000 children (Menon 1979, Singh *et al.* 1982, Kothari 1983a, 1983b, Raja 1993).

(ii) *Stone quarries* in Kerala, Markapur (Andhra Pradesh), and Mandsaur (Madhya Pradesh) employing about 20,000 children (Naidu 1992, ORG 1993).

(iii) *Mines* in Meghalaya employing about 28,000 children.

(iv) *Fishing* in Kerala employing about 20,000 children.

(v) *Handloom* in Trivandrum employing about 10,000 children.

(vi) *Hosiery* in Tirupur (Tamil Nadu) employing about 25,000 to 35,000 children (Venkatramani 1983, Kruijtbosch 1996).

(vii) *Carpet Weaving* in Jammu and Kashmir, Bhadoi, Varanasi and Mirzapur (Uttar Pradesh) employing about 2,00,000 children (Nangia 1988, Vijaygopalan 1993, Raman 1996, National Labour Institute 1993).

(viii) *Pottery Making* in Kashmir and Mirzapur as well as Khurja (Uttar Pradesh) employing about 5,000 children (Singh 1984).

(ix) *Glass Article Making* in Firozabad (Uttar Pradesh) employing about 50,000 children (Giri Institute of Development Studies 1992).

(x) *Gem Polishing* in Jaipur (Rajasthan) employing about 13,000 children (Kruijtbosch 1996, Indian Institute of Health Management Research 1992).

(xi) *Beedi Industries* in Nizamabad District (Andhra Pradesh), North Arcot District (Tamil Nadu) and Gujarat employing about 45,000 children (Jhabvala *et al.* 1991, Pande 1996, Karunanidhi 1995).

(xii) *Brassware Industry* in Moradabad (Uttar Pradesh) employing about 50,000 children (Burra 1989, Kumar and Biswas 1992).

(xiii) *Diamond Industry* in Surat city (Gujarat) employing about 2,00,000 children (ORG 1993, Kanjibhai Desai Samaj Shikshan Bhavan Trust 1997).

(xiv) *Leather Units* of Agra and Kanpur (Uttar Pradesh), Durg (Madhya Pradesh) and Tonk (Rajasthan) employing about 62,000 children (Institute of Applied Manpower Research 1995).

All these major child labour affected sectors are there for long period in India. These sectors along with other child labour affected occupations received attention of Indian government since the British rule. Following are the descriptions of the several official reports as well as commissions, laws and national and international initiatives on child labour in India.

OFFICIAL REPORTS ON CHILD LABOUR IN INDIA

Indian government formed many commissions and committees, to look after the issue of child labour, from the pre-independence era. Each of these commissions/committees brought out detailed reports partially or entirely dealing with child labour situation in India and some of these reports are discussed here.

(a) **Report of the Royal Commission on Labour in India, 1930:** This report observed that most noteworthy effect of the Factories (Amendment) Act, 1922 was that the employment of children in the mills, cotton spinning and weaving industry had reduced though child labourers usually work five hours a day without any interval and sometimes hours of work are often long with unfenced machinery and defective sanitation. Commission also observed that the maximum age limit for the employment of children should be raised to twelve to fourteen years and the employment of children in factories before eight in the morning and after five in the evening should be prohibited.

(b) **Report of the Labour Investigation Committee, 1946:** This Committee under the chairmanship of Mr. D.V. Rege was formed by Government of India to collect data relating to wages and earnings, employment, housing and social conditions of labour in India and to investigate the risks which bring about insecurity, the need of labour to meet such risks and the methods suitable to meet them and the housing and factory conditions.

In its brief mention about child labour the Committee observed that despite the legal provisions, such as the Employment of Children Act (1938), amended in 1939, and sections in the Factories Act and the Indian Mines Act, prohibiting the employment of children below a certain age, their employment continued in some smaller industries: mica splitting, shellac, beedi making, carpet weaving, glass, etc. Committee observes that the children were employed because the income of the family needed supplementing, and the lack of educational facilities would make children idle if they would not join the labour force. Committee suggested that it was need to enforce the legal provisions through proper inspection and provision of educational and other facilities to the children.

(c) **Report of the National Commission on Labour, 1969:** This Commission was formed by the Ministry of Labour in 1966 under the Chairmanship of Dr. P.B. Gajendragadkar to review the conditions of labour and suggest measures for their improvement. The Commission noticed that 8 per cent of the workers were below 15 years of age, with most of them employed in agriculture and the allied activities. The Commission found that in certain industries like glass, beedi, or carpet manufacturing the conditions under which children worked were deplorable. The Commission observed that the employment hours of children should be fixed in such a way so as to enable them to attend school. Where the number of children is adequate, the employers with the assistance of the State Governments should make arrangements to combine work with education.

(d) **Report of the Harbans Singh Committee, 1977:** This Commission was appointed to investigate the problems of child labour in various factories and industries in Ramanathapuram district of Tamil Nadu and the report was submitted in 1977, but was not made public.

(e) **Report of the Committee on Child Labour, 1979:** This Committee under the chairmanship of M.S. Gurupadswamy was formed by the Ministry of Labour to review into detail the causes leading to and the problems arising out of the employment of children in India. The Committee investigated the dimensions of child labour and occupations in which children were employed like in match and fireworks industries, beedi making, glass bangle making, handloom and carpet weaving industry, precious stone polishing industry, in the domestic work, hotels, machine tools and repair shops. The Committee viewed the situation of children in India as one of 'continuing drift'. Bulk of the children continues to be employed in the rural areas. While most of them work without wages, there is an increasing number amongst them employed for wages and also of many working on jobs which are hazardous. The Committee emphasised that unless a systematic evaluation is made from time to time in respect of jobs in which children are employed and certain purposeful policy decisions are taken to meet the deficiencies, the existing situation is not likely to undergo any dimensional, qualitative or quantitative change.

The Committee on detailed examination of the laws dealing with children found that the existing legal framework in this regard is rather inadequate and suggested a single model legislation on child labour in India, such that there are no anomalies on the issues like minimum wages, working hours, medical examination, penalties of offences, etc. It has also suggested to fix the minimum age for entry in the workforce as fifteen years. The Committee also felt the need to involve social workers, voluntary organisations and trade unions as well as parents to assist the enforcement of legislative measures.

(f) **Report on Child Labour in Indian Industries, 1981:** This report is based on a survey conducted by the Labour Bureau in certain organised and unorganised sectors in India. The report presents an account of the various aspects of child labour, e.g., employment, wages and earnings, working conditions, welfare facilities, etc. It was found that in most factories the relevant rules on the hours of work for the children were not adhered to. The report also states that in many hazardous industries like match box, beedi making, repair shops the children were employed and wages paid to the working children in India varied from state to state and industry to industry. The payments were made on piece-rate basis. The report also finds that majority of working children come from poor families to supplement their family income and they are compelled to discontinue their studies as there is no provision of night schools for those who want to continue studies.

CONSTITUTIONAL SAFEGUARDS ON CHILD LABOUR IN INDIA

There are some safeguards in the Constitution of India that have direct and indirect bearings on the problem of child labour which can be discussed as follows:

(i) Article 23—Prohibition of traffic in human beings and forced labour.

(ii) Article 24—Prohibition of employment of children in factories, etc.

(iii) Article 39(e) and 39(f)—Certain principles of policy to be followed by state.

(iv) Article 41—The right to work, to education and to public assistance in particular circumstances.

(v) Article 45—Provision for free and compulsory education for children.

(vi) Article 47—Responsibility of the state to raise the nutritional levels, and standards of living of its citizens and to improve public health.

However, these safeguards have so far proved to be rather inadequate in dealing with the problem of child labour.

LEGAL PROVISIONS ON CHILD LABOUR IN INDIA

Government has also passed several legislations to prevent and/or minimise the exploitation of children in work. These legislations can be chronologically divided into the legislations before independence and after independence.

Legislations before Independence: Major legislations promulgated during British rule which could affect the child labour situation in India can be listed as follows:

(i) *Indian Factories Act, 1881*: It prohibited the employment of children below 7 years in any factory and banned a working period exceeding 9 hours a day.

(ii) *Indian Factories (Amendment) Act, 1891*: It raised the minimum age for work to 9 years and reduced the working period to 7 hours in a day with the prohibition of work at night between 8 p.m. and 5 a.m.

(iii) *The Mines Act, 1901:* It prohibited the employment of children less than 12 years in mines.

(iv) *The Factories Act, 1911:* It prohibited the work by children in factories between 7 p.m. and 5.30 a.m. and in certain dangerous processes.

(v) *The Factories (Amendment) Act, 1922:* It raised the minimum age to 15 years in general, fixed the working hours to a maximum of 6 hours and an interval of half an hour in between, and prohibited the employment of children below 18 in certain processes.

(vi) *The Indian Mines Act, 1923*: The minimum age from 12 to 13 years in mines was raised in the act.

(vii) *The Indian Ports (Amendment) Act, 1931*: It laid 12 years as the minimum age for handling goods in ports.

(viii) *Children (Pledging of Labour) Act, 1933*: This law prohibits parents and guardians from pledging the services of a child. This law was followed in quick succession by the Employment of Children Act, 1938 which has now been replaced by Child Labour (Prohibition and Regulation) Act, 1986.

(ix) *The Factories Act, 1934*: It prohibited the employment of children under 12 years of age and restricted to 5 hours for children between 12 to 15 years.

(x) *The Indian Mines (Amendment) Act, 1935*: It prohibited the employment of children in mines below 15 years of age.

(xi) *Employment of Children Act, 1938*: It sought to prohibit employment of children below 14 years in occupations relating to transport of passengers by rail and in work relating to handling of goods within the limits of any port. The Act fixed the minimum age of employment at 14 years for those engaged in *beedi* making, carpet weaving, cement manufacture, cloth printing, dyeing and weaving, match manufacture, mica cutting, tanning, etc.

Legislations after Independence: After independence, constitutional provisions along with some legislation were made to prevent/minimise the problem of child labour:

(i) *Factories Act, 1948*: Prohibits employment of young children below fourteen years in any factory employing more than 10 persons and using power or employing more than 20 persons where power is not used.

(ii) *The Minimum Wages Act, 1948*: This act provides for an institutional mechanism and procedure for fixation, review, revision, and enforcement of minimum rates of wages.

(iii) *Plantation Act, 1951*: Prohibits the employment of young children below twelve years to work in any plantation. This act also prohibits the children (above 12 years but below 15 years) employed in plantation to work for more than 40 hours a week.

(iv) *Mines Act, 1952*: This act is supposed to prevent the children below fifteen years in any underground or above ground mining operation. This act also has a provision of imprisonment up to three months or a fine up to Rs. 1,000 or both.

(v) *Merchant Shipping Act, 1958*: This act has the provision to prohibit the person under fifteen years of age shall be engaged or carried to sea to work in any capacity in the ships.

(vi) *Motor Transport Workers Act, 1961*: It prohibits children below fifteen years to work in any capacity in any motor transport undertaking.

(vii) *Apprentices Act, 1961*: This act prohibits any person from being engaged as an apprentice unless he is not less than fourteen years of age and satisfies such standards of education and physical fitness as may be prescribed.

(viii) *Beedi and Cigar Workers (Conditions of Employment) Act, 1961*: Under this act no child below 14 years of age can act in beedi and cigar making units irrespective of the number of persons employed.

(ix) *The Bonded Labour System (Abolition) Act, 1975*: This act was introduced with an intention to abolish age-old bonded labour system of India. Government of India has ratified the ILO Convention No. 29 on forced labour in 1954 and the corresponding act on bonded labour was passed in 1996 but made effective from 24 October 1975.

(x) *The Employment of Children (Amendment) Act, 1978*: This amended act included the new clauses which were connected with cinder picking, clearing of ash pits, building operation or connected with the work on railway stations and moving trains were inserted in the former act.

(xi) *Child Labour (Prohibition and Regulation) Act, 1986*: Under this act Government of India prohibited the employment of children in dangerous and hazardous industries and services and regulated their engagement and working conditions in non-hazardous jobs. Though it must be mentioned here that the Act does not use the word 'hazardous' anywhere, the employment of children in certain industries/occupations/processes has been prohibited ostensibly on the ground that they are hazardous and dangerous. This act has an objective to prevent the employment of children in occupations and processes listed in Part A and B of the Schedule of the Act. Through a Notification dated 26-05-1993, the working conditions of children have been regulated in all employments, which are not prohibited under the Act. Through subsequent notifications the Schedule of the Act prohibiting child labour in different occupations and processes has been substantially enlarged bringing the total of 13 occupations and 57 processes respectively. Thus in many important occupations[1] and services[2] in which child labourers are completely prohibited. The regulation provides that a child can work up to maximum of 6 hours a day and 1 hour rest after 3 hours of continuous work. Any employer found during inspections[3] in violation of this act can be punished with 3 to 12 months of rigorous imprisonment or a fine of up to 20,000 rupees or both. Though this law is much more comprehensive than the earlier legislations, there are many gaps and omissions, conceptual, definitional, and operational in the existing law, and these continue to be exploited to the disadvantage of working children and the advantage of unscrupulous elements in industry and commerce. One major shortcoming is the omission of many industries/occupations/processes that may on the face of it appear to harmless or non-hazardous but not quite so when seen closely.[4] Other major criticism can be labelled is the provision regarding 'workshops' by 'occupiers' (meaning those working in premises of manufacturers) with the aid of his family and other purposes. Again a child can work in a prohibited occupation at home along with other members of family as the home of the employed for this purpose is not a 'workshop' of the 'occupier' according to the provision the Act and many manufacturers of beedi or carpets take the opportunity of this shortcoming of the Act by handing over raw materials to the parents who do the manufacturing in their own houses. Similar problems have been faced in regard to determination of the age of the child as according to the provision of this Act the disputes over age should be decided on the basis of a certificate of age provided by the prescribed medical authority to whom such an issue has to be referred for decision and a certificate of age granted by the prescribed medical authority shall for the purpose of the Act be conclusive evidence of the child's age. In India where there is no systematic recording of birth registration, it becomes extremely difficult to correctly determine the age of a child and this provision by the registered medical authority (which took away the court's power to intervene) is leading to many circumventions of Act.

In a recent gazette notification on 2008, Indian Government on the recommendation of the Child Labour Technical Advisory Committee made various amendments of the 1986 Act when they banned the employment of children in some more occupations where the children are exposed to excessive heat and cold like in mechanised fishing, food processing, beverage industry, etc. and exposed to free silica such as slate, pencil industry, stone grinding, etc.

Supreme Court Judgment on Child Labour: The matter regarding elimination of child labour has also been deliberated by the Hon'ble Supreme Court of India. The Supreme Court, in its judgment dated 10th December, 1996 in Writ Petition (Civil) No. 465/1986 has given certain directions regarding the manner in which the children working in the hazardous occupations are to be withdrawn from work and rehabilitated as also the manner in which the working conditions of the children working in non-hazardous occupations are to be regulated and improved upon. The important directions given in the judgment dated 10th December, 1996 include completion of the survey of children working in hazardous employments within a period of six months, payment of compensation amounting to Rs. 20,000 by the offending employer for every child employed in contravention of the provisions of the Act, giving alternative employment to an adult member of the family in place of the child withdrawn from the hazardous occupation or payment of an amount of Rs. 5,000 for each child employed in hazardous employment by the appropriate Government, payment of interest on the corpus of Rs. 25,000 (Rs. 20,000 to be paid by the employer and Rs. 5,000 to be contributed by the appropriate Government) to the family of the child withdrawn from work, provision of education in a suitable institution for the child withdrawn from work and constitution of the Child Labour Rehabilitation-cum-Welfare Fund, constitution of a separate cell in the Labour Department of the appropriate Government for the purpose of monitoring. The implementation of the directions of Supreme Court is being monitored by the Ministry of Labour and compliance of the direction reported to the Hon'ble Court on the basis of information received from the State/UT Governments from time to time.

OTHER NATIONAL INITIATIVES ON CHILD LABOUR IN INDIA

Other national initiatives in India to abolish or minimise the child labour ranged from drafting a national level child labour policy to several endeavours to implement some child labour preventive/prohibitive projects.

National Child Labour Policy: The International Labour Conference adopted a resolution in 1979 on Child Labour. This called for a combination of efforts for prohibition of child labour measures for humanising child labour wherever the same cannot be outrightly eliminated. In deference to the constitutional provisions (Articles 23, 24, 39e & f, 45 and 51c) and in accordance with the letter and spirit of the resolution of 1979 adopted in the International Labour Conference, a National Policy on Child Labour was announced in 1987. The action plan under the National Child Labour Policy comprises of a legislative action plan which seeks to emphasise strict and effective enforcement of the provisions of the Child Labour (Prohibition and Regulation) Act, 1986, the Factories Act, 1948, the Mines Act, 1952, the Plantation Labour Act, 1951, and other Acts containing provisions relating to the employment of children. Focusing of general development programmes for benefiting children wherever possible as various national development programmes exist with wide coverage in the areas of education, health, nutrition, integrated child development, and income and employment generation for the poor.

National Child Labour Projects (NCLP): In pursuance of this policy, the Government of India has been implementing, since 1988 a scheme of National Child Labour Projects (NCLPs) for the rehabilitation of child labour. The major activity undertaken under the NCLP is the establishment of special schools, which provide a package of welfare measures, including non-formal education, skill/craft training, supplementary nutrition, stipend, health care, etc. to children withdrawn from employment. Nine child labour projects were set up in the areas of high concentration of child labour in the year 1988 after the announcement of the National Child Labour Policy, 1987. The number of projects increased to twelve by the middle of 1994.[5] Now there are 100 National Child Labour Projects in 13 child labour endemic States for rehabilitation of approximately 2.11 lakh (.21 million) working children withdrawn from hazardous occupations.

Role of the Voluntary Organisations: NGOs can have an important role to play in the elimination of child labour as they undertake many works regarding this problem like surveying and identifying the child labourers, release of child labourers in the hazardous occupations and rehabilitating them, enhancing awareness among the child labourers' families to dispel misconceptions on the working of children, etc. Central Government of India, under the Grant-in-aid scheme, provides the voluntary organisations with the financial assistance to the extent of 75 per cent of the project cost, for taking up welfare projects for rehabilitation of working children. Financial assistance may also be given for useful and action-oriented research and study on the subject of child labour and preventive measures to discourage further accretion of children into employment. These Grant-in-aid projects are monitored through periodic reports received, field visits, etc. All State Governments are periodically addressed by the Central Government for undertaking comprehensive evaluations of projects.

INTERNATIONAL INITIATIVES ON CHILD LABOUR

International initiatives on child labour consist of conventions and recommendations adopted by the ILO and ratified by member states, IPEC programme by ILO, Convention on the Rights of the Child (CRC) adopted by the General Assembly of UN in 1989 and different initiatives from other UN organisations like UNDP, UNDCP, UNESCO, UNFPA, UNIFEM, UNAIDS, etc.

Some Ratified ILO Conventions: India being an important member state of ILO has ratified many of the significant Conventions adopted by ILO at different times.

Convention No. 5: Minimum Age (Industry) 1919—Ratified on 09-09-1955, it seeks to prohibit employment of children under the age of 14 in any public or private industrial undertaking.

Convention No. 123: Minimum Age (Underground Work) 1965—It was ratified on 20-03-1975 and it has the provision of banning persons under 16 years of age shall not be employed or work in underground mines.

Convention No. 6: Night Work for Young Persons (Industries) 1919—This Convention was ratified on 14-07-1921 and it seeks to abolish the night work for young persons in any public or private industrial undertaking. The provisions of the Convention have been modified for India.

Convention No. 15: Minimum Age (Trimmers Stokers) 1921—Ratified on 20-11-1922, this Convention seeks to prohibit employment of young persons of below 18 years as trimmers and stokers in port. If persons over 18 years are not available then young persons between 16 and 18 can be employed. Trimmers/stokers below 16 years can be employed, subject to medical fitness, in the coastal trade of India.

Convention No. 16: Medical Examination of Young Persons (Sea) 1921—This Convention was ratified on 20-11-1922. It seeks to implement that young person under 18 years of age can be employed on any vessel on the production of a medical certificate attesting fitness for such work.

International Labour Standards and the Core Conventions of ILO: The issue of linkage between world trade and labour standards was first raised at the conclusions of the Uruguay Round at Marrakech in 1994 by the USA. India and other developing countries had taken the position that labour standards at the international levels can be appropriately addressed only in the ILO, not in the WTO as the social clause was not within the mandate of the WTO. In response, India had countered that the relationship between trade and immigration policies may also be examined in the WTO. The issue again came up at the First Ministerial Conference of the WTO in Singapore in 1996. In this Conference, developing countries including India once again rejected the proposal of the US to include labour standards as an agenda in the WTO. The final Ministerial Declaration at Singapore endorsed the stand of the developing countries and reiterated that ILO is the competent body to set and deal with core labour standards and the WTO and ILO Secretariats would continue their existing collaboration. It also rejected the use of labour standards for protectionist purposes and agreed that the comparative advantage of countries, particularly low wage developing countries, must in no way be put into question.

In the Third WTO Ministerial Conference held in Seattle in 1999, the US had proposed establishment of a Working Group on Trade and Labour, which would deal with issues such as trade and employment, trade and social protection, core labour standards, forced and child labour, etc. and submits a report for consideration at the Fourth Ministerial Conference. The European Union proposed the establishment of a joint ILO-WTO Working Forum on trade, globalisation and labour issues to promote better understanding of the issues involved through a substantial dialogue between all interested parties including governments, employers, trade unions and other international organisations. There was no conclusive outcome from this Conference, which attracted much criticism and demonstrations by NGOs and other activist groups. The Fourth Ministerial Conference of the WTO, which was held in Doha from 9th to 14th November 2001, reaffirmed the Declaration made at the Singapore Ministerial Conference of the WTO that ILO is the appropriate forum to set and deal with the issues of core labour standards.

Since its inception, the primary task of ILO is the setting up the International Labour Standards in the form of Conventions and Recommendations. Conventions are international treaties and are instruments, which create legally binding obligations on the countries to ratify them. Recommendations are, however, non-binding and set out guidelines orienting national policies and actions.

There are eight core conventions which ILO termed as fundamental/human rights conventions. Indian government has ratified four of those conventions but did not ratify the four other for various reasons. The four ratified conventions are:

(i) Forced Labour Convention (Convention No. 29)

(ii) Abolition of Forced Labour Convention (Convention No. 105)

(iii) Equal Remuneration Convention (Convention No. 100)

(iv) Discrimination (Employment Occupation) Convention (Convention No. 111).

The four non-ratified conventions are:

(i) Freedom of Association and Protection of Right to Organised Convention (No. 87)

(ii) Right to Organise and Collective Bargaining Convention (No. 98)

(iii) Minimum Age Convention (No. 138)

(iv) Worst forms of Child Labour Convention (No. 182).

Consequent to the World Summit for Social Development in 1995, the above-mentioned Conventions (Convention Nos. 29, 105, 100, 111, 87, 98, and 138) were categorised as the Fundamental Human Rights Conventions or Core Conventions by the ILO. Later on, Convention No. 182 [Sl. No. viii above] was added to the list. As per the Declaration on Fundamental Principles and Rights at Work and its Follow-up, each Member State of the ILO is expected to give effect to the principles contained in the Core Conventions of the ILO, irrespective of whether or not the Core Conventions have been ratified by them.

Conventions No. 87 and 98: Convention No. 87 provides for the right of workers and employers, without any distinction to establish and join organisations of their own choosing without previous authorisation. Their organisations have the right to form or join federations and confederations, including on the international level. Convention No. 98 aims to protect the exercise of the right to organise and to promote voluntary collective bargaining. According to the Indian Government, the guarantees provided for under these two Conventions are by and large available to workers in India by means of constitutional provisions, laws and regulations and practices. Though the freedom of expression, freedom of association and functional democracy are guaranteed by our Constitution and there are some alternative grievance redress mechanisms like Joint Consultative Machinery, Central Administrative Tribunal, etc.; it seems unlikely that without the ratification of these two convention the rights of the workers like job security, social security and fair working conditions and fair wages are fully safe in our country.

Convention No. 138: Convention No. 138 (1973) which stipulates the minimum age of entry to employment in accordance with this convention is 13 years for light work and 18 years for hazardous work, is probably the most comprehensive ILO Convention on child labour. According to the Indian Government, this Convention has not been ratified as for ratifying Convention No. 138, enactment of a suitable all encompassing Central Legislation in India for minimum age of entry to employment would need to be enacted. Again, the definition of 'child' in all concerned existing legislations would then need to be determined in accordance with the provisions of the Central Legislation on minimum age for admission to employment. Thus, the Bill on the above lines on its enactment is going to cause redrafting of the concerned existing legislations like the Child Labour (Prohibition and Regulation) Act, 1986, etc.

Convention No. 182: Ratification of Convention No. 182 [Geneva International Labour Conference (87th Session) in June 1999] concerning Worst Forms of Child Labour is being pursued by the ILO with all member countries including India. This Convention currently proposes to prohibit four categories of child labour:

(i) Slavery and similar practices, including sale and trafficking of children.

(ii) The commercial sexual exploitation of children.

(iii) Hazardous work jeopardising a child's health, safety and morals, and

(iv) Involvement in other illegal activities such as drug trafficking.

The Recommendation suggests that all categories except hazardous work should be classified as criminal offences. In defining hazardous work, consideration should be given to "work...for long hours, during the night or without the possibility of returning home each day".

Other Major International Initiatives: Other major international initiatives to abolish child labour in India include:

(i) **Convention on the Rights of the Child** (CRC): It was adopted by the General Assembly of UN in 1989 and ratified by 191 countries including India. CRC happens to be the most comprehensive treaty on the rights of children whom it defines as 'persons under the age of eighteen unless age of majority is attained earlier'. It seeks to protect a wide range of children's rights, including the right to be protected from economic exploitation and from performing any work that is likely to be hazardous or to interfere with their education or to be harmful to their health or physical, mental, spiritual, moral, or social development. Ratification of this treaty made the state responsible for and obligation to respect, protect, facilitate and fulfil the rights embodied in the CRC as the CRC requires state parties to take legislative, administrative, social, and educational measures to ensure the implementation of the Convention:

(a) By specifying a minimum age or minimum age for admission to employment,

(b) By promulgating appropriate regulation of the hours of work and conditions of employment, and

(c) By levying appropriate penalties or other sanctions to ensure the effective enforcement of its provisions.

The CRC also contains important provisions that have a bearing on worst forms of child labour particularly in the Third World such as the sexual exploitation of children and the abduction and sale and trafficking of children for any purpose or in any form.

(ii) IPEC (International Programme on the Elimination of Child Labour): It was established by ILO in 1992 for a global technical cooperation on child labour. The implementation of IPEC programmes in India has certainly created a very positive impact towards understanding the problem of child labour and in highlighting the need to elimination child labour as expeditiously as possible. The major contribution of the IPEC programme in India has been the generating of a critical consciousness among all the social partners for taking corrective measures to eliminate child labour. Major achievements of IPEC in India, as claimed by the agencies, include:

- Rehabilitation of about one lakh (0.1 million) working children employed in hazardous and other extremely adverse conditions across the country.
- Motivating as well as sensitising the trade unions and

the employers with their organisations against child labour.

- Making government, quasi-government and non-government agencies, autonomous bodies, etc. aware about the gravity of the child labour situation in India.
- Conducting research studies to understand the implications of child labour and documenting them.
- Setting up of a Child Labour Cell in the National Institute of Rural Development (NIRD), Hyderabad to assist the central and state governments in introducing policy changes to combat in the rural areas.
- Developing training packages to promote sustainable income generation activities for mothers of children rehabilitated from work to substitute the fall in family incomes on account of withdrawal of the child from work.

(iii) **International Labour Conference (86th Session) on 1998:** At this conference ILO brought out the Report VI(1) called 'Child Labour: Targeting the Intolerable'. The report stressed on nine important factors, namely:

1. A new Convention on child labour.
2. Time-bound programme of action to eliminate child labour.
3. Immediate suppression of extreme forms of child labour.
4. Prohibition of work for the very young (under 12 or 13 years) and special protection for girls.
5. Rehabilitation to ensure permanent removal from hazardous work.
6. Preventive measures.
7. Designation of national authority responsible for child labour.
8. Making crime against a child anywhere a crime everywhere.
9. Increased financial aid to fight against child labour.

(iv) **Social Labelling of Child Labour Products:** This kind of labelling is often referred to as voluntary social labelling and it is one of the most frequently used ways in the Western countries to prevent child labour. Social labels are actually intended to inform consumers about the social conditions of production, in order to assure them that the item they are about to purchase was produced under fair and equitable working conditions. This puts pressure on producers to introduce such conditions. The proponents of most social labelling initiatives concerning child labour, for example, are trying to initiate change by starting from the consumer and moving back through the marketing chain to affect modes of production and improve the lives of working children, either by pressing for the complete removal of child labourers from the production process or the amelioration of their working and living conditions. These labelling initiatives usually have another aim as well: that of directly contributing to improvements in the situation of child labourers and their families and communities by setting up local projects financed through the labelling initiative itself. Therefore, according to the supporters of social labelling, it has some economic components. All voluntary social labelling initiatives currently in existence share at least the following features:

- The physical labelling of certain products, or of the retail establishments that offer these products for sale to the public, by using either a descriptive label or a logo that has a specific social meaning for its sponsors.
- The label or logo implies that certain standards have been met concerning the social conditions in which these products were produced.
- The labelling initiatives necessitate outreach towards consumers, in order to communicate to them the importance and social implications of purchasing the labelled products rather than others.
- The relation between labelling and social standards requires some form of oversight function in order to ensure that the social standards that are the object of labelling have actually been realised or are being maintained in the countries of production.

- The labelling initiative collects funds (a levy) from the retailers or importers of the products in order to improve specific conditions in the region of production. These levies are usually a very small percentage of the sales volume or import volume of the product, and may increase the actual unit price of the product to consumers by up to two per cent.

All these social labelling initiatives (there are six major child labour labelling initiatives) are supposed to improve the situation of child labourers. According to various observers in the field of child labour, social labelling with reference to child labour is only regarded as one of the possible interventions to eliminate child labour in a country or region. Labelling only helps, if at all, as part of a series of activities articulated within a broader policy and strategy. This approach has proved somewhat counter-productive for various reasons like the vested interests of the local or outside stakeholders going against this Western intervention. Thus individuals, groups and certain commercial communities see social labelling as one form of restraint of trade, namely the imposition of social costs. But the restraint of freedom in the pursuit and practice of business and the mistrust between the labeller and labelled are the major deterrents for a successful labelling initiative.

The author would also like to mention some other international efforts having effects on the child labour situation in India like Child Labour Action and Support Programmes (CLASP) funded by ILO, South Asia Poverty Alleviation Programme funded by UNDP, Programme for Street Children funded by UNDCP, Learning Without Frontiers (LWF) Programme funded by UNESCO, Support activities in the context of the Government of India's Adult Literacy Programme run by UNFPA, Entrepreneurship Development Programme for Women funded by UNIFEM, Activities on Child Trafficking funded by UNAIDS, UN System Support for Community-based Primary Education, Child Labour Conferences in February 1997 in Amsterdam and in October 1997 in Oslo, International Labour Conference (86th Session) in 1998[6] and Geneva International Labour Conference (87th Session) in June 1999.[7]

Thus one can find that various national as well as international initiatives fought the problem of child labour but these initiatives singly or in conjunction with the other initiatives proved to be adequate to eradicate and/or ameliorate this problem in the Third World countries including India. This work reveals that there a dearth of culturally relative assessments of the Third World populations where the problem and this lack of culturally relative assessments is one of the major reasons of this failure.

NOTES

1. Major child labour prohibited occupations include transport, cinder picking and clearing ash-pit in railway sideways and workshops, working in catering establishment in railway station or as vendors or in any establishment where the work involves moving one platform to another or within a moving train or outside, building railway station or in any work near railway station or between the railway lines, any work inside a port area, and in any temporarily licensed explosive and fireworks shops.
2. Major child labour prohibited services include beedi making, carpet weaving, cement manufacture and bagging of cement, cloth printing, dyeing and weaving, manufacture of matches, explosives and fireworks, soap manufacturing, wool cleaning, building and construction industry, manufacture of slate pencil, shellac manufacture, tanning and manufacture of leather goods, mica-cutting and splitting, diamond cutting and gem polishing, and any manufacturing industry where the following poisonous elements are used like—lead, mercury, manganese, chromium, benzene, pesticides and asbestos.
3. According to ILO (1998: 112) difficulties encountered by labour inspectorates are manifold which include lack of material resources including scarce transport, understaffing of inspection offices, overwork and low pay for inspectors, inspectors' perception of child labour, lack of appropriate training on the special vulnerability of children, child labour and hazards to which children are exposed, powers limited by law and lack of appropriate techniques, lack of motivation, hostile environment, lack of cooperation and support from other government agencies, including the education system, and clandestine nature of child work.

4. Recently, in August, 2006, Indian government has included domestic work in the list of hazardous work for the children and banned the employing child labour in domestic sector.
5. Nine NCLPs started in areas of high concentration of child labour are:
   (a) Match, fireworks, and explosive industry in Sivakasi in Tamil Nadu.
   (b) Precious stone polishing industry in Jaipur in Rajasthan.
   (c) Glass and bangles industry in Ferozabad in Uttar Pradesh.
   (d) Brassware industry in Moradabad in Uttar Pradesh.
   (e) Handmade carpet industry in Mirzapur, Varanasi, and Bhadoi in Uttar Pradesh.
   (f) Lock-making industry in Aligarh in Uttar Pradesh.
   (g) Tile industry in Jagampet in Andhra Pradesh.
   (h) Slate industry in Markapur in Andhra Pradesh.
   (i) Slate industry in Mandsaur in Madhya Pradesh.

   Subsequently NCLP were launched in Sambalpur, Thane, and Gharwa.
6. In this session ILO brought out the Report VI(1) called 'Child Labor: Targeting the Intolerable'. The report stressed on nine important factors, namely:
   (a) A new Convention on child labour.
   (b) Time-bound programme of action to eliminate child labour.
   (c) Immediate suppression of extreme forms of child labour.
   (d) Prohibition of work for the very young (under 12 or 13 years) and special protection for girls.
   (e) Rehabilitation to ensure permanent removal from hazardous work.
   (f) Preventive measures.
   (g) Designation of national authority responsible for child labour.
   (h) Making crime against a child anywhere a crime everywhere.
   (i) Increased financial aid to fight against child labour.
7. In this conference ILO adopted Convention No. 182 which is more specific than the Convention No. 138.

3

Design, Results and Analyses

SECTION I—OUTLINING THE RESEARCH DESIGN

As indicated earlier, there is not one likely cause of child labour, nor can any single model adequately explain a complex phenomenon like it. Several factors both at the household level like low income and wealth (Jensen 1999), income instability and spiralling debt (Jensen 1999, 2000), large family size causing less investment in child upbringing (Butcher and Case 1992, Garg and Morduch 1998), vulnerable household structure and migration (Jensen 1999) and indifferent parental perceptions, attitudes and aspirations on the children's future (Jensen 1999) and some external factors like inappropriate nature of schools (Case and Deaton 1999, Jensen 1999, 2000), demand for child labour by employers of formal and informal enterprises or in family farms, socio-economic attitudes towards children and work as well as legislative factors are cited as the causes of child labour.

As an anthropologist, the author began his search at the most basic level i.e. the household level as the households make decisions regarding how children's time will be allocated between leisure, schooling, household activities and employment. For an anthropologist, the key here is to consider the household not in isolation, but to realise that decisions are made within a context, and are influenced by factors external to the household like the level of marginality in terms of the accessibility of households to the basic facilities of life like school, housing condition, security of tenure of the houses, etc., the demand for child labour, the legal and cultural contexts barring/favouring child labour, and international factors like globalisation affecting the Third World economy. During this research on child labour, author found the presence of a complex interaction among these factors acting at different levels and felt that only a 'holistic' view on the problem can facilitates a proper understanding of the phenomenon.

During this fieldwork, the author tried to examine the relationship of the phenomenon of child labour with the poverty and aspects of vulnerability of the households. It involved close scrutiny of several parameters of the household like incidences of unemployment in the family, types of the primary occupation, system of receiving payment of wage or income, level of daily income, level of monthly savings, cost of living, etc. In this research design, the author also tried to incorporate issues like the family composition and parental perception of children. Along with the size of the individual families the author also studied various related aspects like type of the family, child-woman ratios, old age dependency ratio, age at marriage, standard of education, overall literacy, child literacy, etc. Parental perceptions on the work/education of their children were studied qualitatively employing techniques like case study, studying key behaviours and observing socially cognisant items among the populations under study.

Having discussed the issues at the household level the author found it imperative to extend his research design to the factors which exist outside the household level and the individuals in the household level have little or no control over those factors. As explained earlier, there are a number of factors outside the household that can affect the child labour situation. From his fieldwork experience on child labour in Kolkata, the author found that the conditions of urban marginality in terms of individual's accessibility to the basic amenities of life (also called as collective consumption) like school, living condition of the household, security of tenure of the settlement, etc.; the demand for child labour; the efficacy of legal and other initiatives to prevent child labour and cultural contexts on child labour; and the international factors like globalisation affecting the Third World economy are the important components to be studied if one wants to explain the phenomenon of child labour in the Third World.

The *selection of a particular population or site* in anthropological researches has ordinarily related to some unanswered questions or outstanding problems in the body of comparative anthropological theory. Personal predilections or connections of researchers also shapes this selection, but a fieldworker still must justify his or her choice in terms of some significant theory to which the project is addressed. In this work, the fieldsites were selected in a manner which allowed the author to engage in a long-term research in more than one urban fieldsite (more precisely three fieldsites) in Kolkata for comparison purposes. Thus three populations were selected on the basis of their differential positions on urban marginality in the city of Kolkata. First two populations (i.e. Population-I and Population-II) were 'illegally' constructed squatter settlements where the residents did not have any security of tenure on the land they were living. Population-I was selected on the basis of the information of an impending eviction of the settlement as a part of the proposed widening of a road. This settlement was selected to initiate a study on urban marginalisation in a Third World city and thus the selection of the Population-I can be regarded as an extreme case selection. The selection of Population-II was done with a view to conduct a long-term study among the marginalised people in urban setting with no security of tenure and with little or no urban amenities (or collective consumption). The largest stretch of squatter population during the time of this fieldwork on the two sides of the Beliaghata Circular Canal the city of Kolkata fulfilled this criterion. The selection of the aforesaid stretch was done after some preliminary studies in some other stretches of these canal-side dwellers and after some explorations the author found the studied stretch as an ideal one for study due to various reasons like more congenial atmosphere for fieldwork, presence of meaningful contacts, presence of willing informants, etc. Population-III, on the other, was a recognized slum population for more than two decades where the residents were living (and in fact still living) with some kind of security of tenure in the form of Thika Tenancy Act under which they could live on the land but were unable to sell. Population-III served as an ideal setting for studying the outcome of providing security of tenure to the marginalised people in the city of Kolkata. This slum has been the beneficiary of most of the urban development programmes meant for providing shelter and other basic services to the urban poor since the settlement and its inhabitants possessed permanent addresses—a prerequisite for initiating these development programmes. This slum settlement was selected on the basis of these criteria and was considered as the Programme Group since it received the programme in the form of security of tenure over a period of time. Population-I and Population-II (called here as Population-I and II), in combination, constituted the Control Group in this study as these two settlements had not benefited from the programme in the form of security of tenure like Population-III.

The next major task during this fieldwork was to *gain entry in the fieldsites* where, in most cases, the local contacts were used. The author used to carry his identity documents all along the fieldwork and always let the local contacts introduce him to the people in all the fieldsites. Some introductory statements on the motive, use of the fieldwork for the population under study, etc. always proved to be very useful during this fieldwork. Even though the process of initial contact went smoothly, the author frequently felt that the act of fieldwork is a fairly turbulent process. As Bernard (1988, 164-65) puts it, "some form of depression and shock thereafter (within a week or two). One kind of shock comes as the novelty of the field site wears off and there is this nasty feeling that anthropology has to get done. Another kind of shock is to the culture itself. Culture shock is an uncomfortable stress response, and must be taken very seriously." During this fieldwork, the author experienced those shocks and sometimes even had to take some temporary breaks in his fieldwork to let the shock be somewhat absorbed. At times *rapport building* in this fieldwork proved to be very difficult as the nature of this research did not always permitted the author to spend much time with the informants for rapport building. Hence at many occasions the author avoided asking for 'meaning' of a particular fact, instead he frequently enquired on the 'use' as meaning emerged from the repeated observation or participant observation of the facts or events. During the *selection of informants* the author always kept a few factors in mind like enculturation of the person concerned, his/her representativeness in the population, articulating power, capability of following the method of investigation and the persons who could act as intermediaries in this research. During this fieldwork open-ended semi-structured interviewing was most useful in most of the situations. During the *selection a key informant* in this fieldwork, the author used to look for some additional factors in a potential key informant like knowledge about the topic of interest, involved in the domain of interest or recently experienced, informant's ability to contemplate, staying around in the population for a while and a person with whom the author could develop a kind of social relationship. Key informant interviewing techniques in this fieldwork included iteration of the previous interview, providing probing stimuli, posing leading questions, rephrasing incomprehensible questions, using informant responses and keeping provision of further meeting. In many cases the author used to let the key informants select the settings for interview and mostly recorded these key interviews as written notes as well as in tape recorders. Informal interviews, semi-structured interviews and standardised open-ended interviews all were in use in different phases during the key interviewing during this fieldwork.

The author has compiled many of his findings of this fieldwork as *non-participant observer* i.e. by spending more time in the field-setting to collect observation data without significantly interacting with the subjects. Most of the non-participant observations used during this fieldwork were unstructured focused observation especially during the initial exploratory part of this study and structured observation as an effort to quantify the record of some of the key behaviours. On the other hand, there were many observations conducted during this fieldwork that were participatory in nature which had been enhanced by staying with the informants and participating as much as possible in their daily lives. As we know that this form of unobtrusive-unstructured form of observation is considered as the *sine qua non* of any long-term ethnography. In this fieldwork, a good deal of time and rapport-building became necessary before informants stopped noticing the novelty of fieldworker's presence as a researcher and participation, and could go about their daily routine without inhibitions. Moreover, the author tried to attend the ethics of information gathering and possessing information about the daily activities of people who might come to think of the participant observer as more of a participant than an observer, with the attendant level of confidence that produces. *Participant observation* in this fieldwork mostly went along the scheme of 'speech-in-action' where situational continuum usually ranges from the informant's turf—finding the informants where they are—and the ethnographer's turf and control. The author would like to mention here that the 'speech-in-action' followed (though not literally) during the key informant interviewing, in most cases, ended in the shared control stage. The author was somewhat deliberate in this regard due to the specific nature of these fieldsites.

Free lists and ranking were used during this fieldwork to determine and rank the socially cognizant items among the people under study. Case study was another frequently employed method used in this fieldwork. Case study proved to be very useful during the advanced stages of the fieldwork when the relationship with informants grew considerably and the informant was on the researcher's turf with control share or the researcher in control. *Data analysis* in any anthropological work, including this one, took place throughout the time-span of the research work as it refined our ideas on our research goals. However, at the last stage of the research work, like other anthropologists, the author became fully involved with the analysis of the data collected from the fieldwork. In this fieldwork major ways of data analysis consisted of repeated reading of fieldnotes, interview transcripts, site documents, etc., marking the data, eliciting 'insiders' points of view, testing categories and explanations and triangulation among the various forms of data. With this research design the author tried to gather data from his field which might actually induce a paradigm shift as the current theories, definitions and conceptions could not properly explain findings from this field.

SECTION II—PROFILE OF THE POPULATIONS

This research, in its pursuit of a Third Worldly understanding of the child labour problem in an urban situation, selected three populations in Kolkata primarily on the basis of their conditions of urban marginality in terms of urban space and on the availability of state mediated/provided urban amenities. Thus Population-I and Population-II in this research frame were squatter settlements or *jhaupris* which did not have any security of tenure, i.e. people living in these settlements did not hold title to the lands and/or their housing structure. Population-III, on the other hand, was a slum or *bustee* settlement where the government subsequently authorised the settlers' right to live on the land under Calcutta Thika and Other Tenancies and Land (Acquisition and Regulation) Act, 1981. But they cannot sell their property as the ownership of structure has been separated from the land and it is the *Thika* or *bustee* dwellers who own the structure. Thus, according to this research design, Population-III (which received the programme in form of a kind of security of tenure of their housing structure under the above-mentioned act) was regarded as the Programme Group or Treatment Group. The other two populations i.e. Population-I and Population-II (in this book they were in combination called as Population-I and II) were regarded as the Control Group or Comparison Group as they did not received this programme i.e. the security of tenure of their housing structure before their evictions and were not by any means protected under any law or act. Initially the author treated the data of all three populations separately and then merged the data of Population-I and Population-II (as mentioned earlier, the combined population has been termed here as the Population-I and II) as it would be revealed when one goes through those data separately that the findings in both the Population-I and Population-II were almost identical. Subsequently, the data of the Population-I and II (i.e. the Control Group) were compared here with the data of the Programme Group i.e. the Population-III.

The author would like to begin the discussions on the empirical findings by considering the *age and sex-wise distribution* (Table 3.10.1) of these people which reveals that the profile of all the studied urban marginalised people were largely dominated by the younger population, i.e. persons up to 14 years of age and these younger persons together constituted 46.21 per cent of the total population. At the same time, the presence of the persons of over the age of 45 years was remarkably low, i.e. only 17.84 per cent of the total population. This declining trend of the presence of older people was particularly discernible among the female section of these populations. These are the typical features of the marginalised people in a Third World urban scenario like Kolkata. Likewise, it has been evident that the profiles of the Control Group populations would reflect similar features like higher proportion of persons below 15 years of age, very low presence of persons over the age of 45 years (especially the females of over 45 years) and the data of both the populations bear some remarkable resemblances in each age group for both the genders.

In similarity with the overall trends, the data of the Control Group have shown that persons in all the three age-groups below 15 years (i.e. 0-4 years, 5-9 years, and 10-14 years) accounted for more than half of the total population (52.96 per cent). Hence it would be not surprising to note that in the Control Group, the highest proportion of the persons was found in the age-group 0-4 years (18.81 per cent) followed by the age group 5-9 years (18.00 per cent) and the age group 10-14 years (16.15 per cent). This factor might be attributed to the high crude birth rate[1] in the Control Group, calculation of which is beyond the scope of this study. It might also indicate a high total fertility rate[2] in the Control Group which was again not calculable during this study. However, the Indian picture at large and the picture of Kolkata in particular would give the similar indications to this high total fertility rate.[3] The author resorted to the calculation of the child-woman ratios for both the age groups of 0-4 years and 5-9 years in place of the fertility rate to have an idea on the fertility trends of these two populations. The author tried to study the trend of infant mortality as a high infant mortality rate was expected among the people of the Control Group. But the lack of any proper child death registration system made the study on infant mortality rate impossible among the Control Group. However, during this research all the available female informants in reproductive age (i.e. 15-49 years) were asked about the children they gave birth to but could not complete their first year of birth. The impression that the author gathered that a substantial proportion of these women from the Control Group passed through the traumatic experiences of seeing one or more of their children dead within the first year of their birth.[4]

> **Case Study No. 1 (Population-II):** 'I am Gudia Begum... aged 29...living here for the last ten years.... I came to this settlement after my marriage. I have two sons, one is seven years old other is on my lap...one year old. I work as a scrap-sorter now. Earlier I used to work in the houses (as a domestic help). I had to leave that work few years back when I lost my second child.... It was a boy. He was suffering from a urinary disease. I went to many doctors, Pir Baba and local quacks, and gave many medicines to that child. We spend lots of money behind that treatment.... He died in spite of every effort...at the age of few months...at about the ninth months of age.... I have also gave birth to a dead child before the birth of my first child. Everybody consoled me at that time and told me to keep faith in Allah. I took some medicines given by the Pir Baba and (I believe) my first child was born thereafter....'

Actually this declining trend in the frequency of surviving women started right from the age group 40-44 years where the frequency was 5.09 per cent compared to 7.70 per cent in the earlier age group 35-39 years. The sharp fall of population was more noticeable in the age group 45-49 which reached to as low as 2.89 per cent of the total population. The declining trend continued in the next age group 50-54 years (2.20 per cent), and finally culminated in age groups of 55-59 years and 60+ years which had the smallest shares of the total population. This phenomenon of the sharp decline of population with increasing age after 40 years of age particularly for female population was an indicative of low life expectancy and higher mortality of people (particularly among the females) in the Control Group after 40 years of age among these people.

On the other hand, the age and sex-wise distribution in the Programme Group reveals many contrasting features. Thus one can find that the persons below 15 years (i.e. merging the population in the age groups of 0-4, 5-9 and 10-14 years) consisted of 25.50 per cent. This is a lower proportion of the population that found in the corresponding age group in the Control Group. It would indicate lower birth rate in the Programme Group. Again child-woman ratio would offer some more insights to this phenomenon in the Programme Group.

As indicated earlier, in the absence of any data on total fertility rate the author resorted to child woman ratio (CWR) among these people. This ratio is primarily defined as the presence of the number of children per 1000 women in reproductive age. The ratio is calculated among the children of two age groups namely, 0-4 years and 5-9 years.

(a) *Child Woman Ratio of the Age Group 0-4 years [CWR (0-4)]* is defined as number of children of age 0-4 years per 1000 women aged 15-49 years. In this study CWR (0-4) (Table 3.10.2) of All Populations (641 children per 1000 women aged 15-49 years) was higher than the national level as well as the state level in the urban setting.[5] In the Control Group this ratio was even higher (834 children per 1000 women aged 15-49 years).[6] On a closer look it was found that in Population-I, CWR (0-4) was particularly high (1321 children per 1000 women aged 15-49 years). On the other hand the CWR (0-4) in the Programme Group was much lower (210 children per 1000 women aged 15-49 years), even lower than the national and the state levels in this regard and thus reflecting a much better quality of life of the children as well as of the mothers in the Programme Group.

(b) *Child Woman Ratio of the Age Group 5-9 years [CWR (5-9)]* is defined as number of children of age 5-9 years per 1000 women aged 15-49 years. Here again the CWR (5-9) of All Populations was high (615 children per 1000 women aged 15-49 years) and exceeded the national and the state levels in urban areas.[7] In the Control Group the CWR (5-9) was very high (798 children per 1000 women aged 15-49 years).[8] By contrast CWR (5-9) in the Programme Group was much lower (277 children per 1000 women aged 15-49 years), even lower than the national and the state levels in urban setting (see Table 3.10.3).

If we compare the CWR (0-4) and CWR (5-9) (Table 3.10.4) among all these people we would find that both the CWR (0-4) and CWR (5-9) were particularly high i.e. more than double the national and the state levels, in Population-I. In Population-II both these ratios were half that of the Population-I value. In the Programme Group both the ratios were much lower than the national and the state level. In All Populations both CWR (0-4) and CWR (5-9) were comparatively higher than the national and the state levels. The contrasting features of CWR (0-4) and CWR (5-9) of the two groups of population can be explained in the backdrop of marginalisation of population in a Third World city like Kolkata where owing to the absence of family planning facilities these marginalised sections of population have failed to limit the number of their children. As a result of the increased number of children, their family size grows without any corresponding increase in family income. Thus the problem compounds among the marginalised people leading to a further worsening condition and forces them to undertake many survival strategies which include the releasing of their children in the workforce at a tender age as found in the Control Group. On the other hand, the Programme Group had tackled this problem somewhat better and the trends there as far as the family size is much better than the Control Group.

SECTION III—EDUCATIONAL ASPECTS OF THE POPULATIONS

The author has explored the educational aspects of the studied populations (children and adults alike) with much importance as some observers believe that it is one of the major causes of child labour. The *distribution of these populations according to the standard of education* (Table 3.10.5) has indicated that as high as 28.66 per cent of All Populations were non-literates[9] and most of these non-literate persons were females (22.95 per cent). As high as 19.67 per cent of these people were able to 'sign their names only' in their respective languages which again in reality could not taken as a *de facto* literacy as most of them could hardly read or write anything else than their individual names. Nearly 15 per cent (15.50 per cent) of All Populations had read up to class IV while 10.55 per cent had read up to class VIII and 4.38 per cent up to class X. But very few (2.85 per cent) actually passed the Madhyamik or Secondary School Leaving examination. Even fewer (1.59 per cent) proportions of All Populations had actually passed the Higher Secondary level (High School Level) and the frequency of passing the graduation level was negligible (0.74 per cent). In the Control Group the picture was even grimmer as 35.85 per cent of this population were non-literates and 22.54 per cent were 'able to sign their names only'. Another 14.35 per cent were reported to have read up to the primary level (class I-IV) followed by the 5.80 per cent who had completed education up to class V to VIII. There were very few (0.72 per cent) persons (all were males) who were reported to have passed the School Final level (Madhyamik/Secondary level in West Bengal) and none was reported to have read beyond that level. This educational scenario reflects a lower literacy rate[10] than either at the national or the state level (both in combined and urban settings).[11] On the other hand, the Programme Group presents completely contrasting picture with much fewer persons who were either non-literates (7.45 per cent) or 'could sign their names only' (10.90 per cent). Many of this population actually crossed the secondary level (9.66 per cent) as well as the higher secondary level (6.48 per cent) of education. Some of them even passed the graduation and/or the higher level of education (2.90 per cent) which was a remarkable phenomenon considering the lack of opportunities available to this section of urban population. It might be mentioned here that according to this distribution, the females of this population were found to be less well educated. This trend is exemplified by the presence of more female not-literates (5.65 per cent females compared to 1.79 per cent males in this category), fewer females with secondary level education (3.44 per cent females compared to 6.21 per cent males in this category), higher secondary level of education (0.83 per cent females compared to 5.65 per cent males in this category) and in some other categories. These findings have corroborated the other findings on the overall low status of women in the Programme Group even though the overall situation was remarkably improved here.

The distribution of these people *according to overall literacy* (Table 3.10.6) has revealed that in All Populations the literacy rate[12] was only 54.08 per cent which was much lower than the national[13] and the state average[14] as per the Census of India (2001) and the earlier calculations by 53rd round NSSO calculations.[15] The gender-wise distribution showed that in All Populations, the male literacy rate was 71.77 per cent and the female literacy rate of 35.78 per cent which were again far below the national and state levels according to the 2001 census data[16] and the NSSO data[17] in the combined areas and in the urban areas. In the Control Group the literacy situation was worse as only 44.08 per cent were literates with male literacy rate was 67.31 per cent but the female literacy rate was only 21.15 per cent. On the other hand, the Programme Group had a completely different picture in this regard. The literacy rate (78.97 per cent) was much nearer to the national and the state levels of literacy in the urban areas. Gender-wise distribution of the literacy rate in the Programme Group also showed similar picture with a male literacy rate was 82.28 per cent and female literacy rate of 75.40 per cent which was higher than the national level.

Distribution of population *according to child literacy rate*[18] (Table 3.10.7) showed that 54.27 per cent of the children were literates—both more than the child literacy rate at the national and the state level.[19] 78.91 per cent of the male children and 29.01 per cent of the female children in All Populations were literate. Child literacy rate was only 46.75 per cent in the Control Group. Though the male child literacy rate was somewhat better (74.63 per cent which was even slightly higher than the national as well as the state level), the female child literacy rate was very low (19.86 per cent which was much lower than the national and the state level)[20] and thus affecting the overall child literacy rate. In the Control Group most of the girl children were either non-literates or 'could sign their names only' and very few of them had actually passed the primary level of education. This worsened female child literacy rate was primarily due to the low status of women in a society where the girls are predominantly seen as the burdens on their parents.

> **Case Study No. 2 (Population-I):** 'My name is Farah, my age is 10 years...I am living in this settlement since my birth...I have two brothers...one is elder than me and the other is younger.... I can sign my name in Urdu...I learnt to read Kalma (Arabic verses of Koran).... I read for few days in a nearby Madrasa school but my parents withdrew me from that school.... Yes, my elder brother still reads in a nearby school and my younger brother is yet to be grown enough to be admitted in the school.... Now I act as a scrap-picker and sometimes as a scrap-sorter.... After returning from the work I help my mother in the household activities....'

On the other hand, in the Programme Group the child literacy rate was as high as 95.10 per cent with vastly improved female child literacy rate (90.48 per cent) and almost full literacy among the male children (98.33 per cent). This picture is congruent with the overall improved nature of the women status in the Programme Group. Here, girls were much better looked after even though they were not viewed as an asset for their families.

> **Case Study No. 3 (Population-III):** 'I am Sikha Adhikary, my age is 11 years. I am living in this settlement since my birth.... I read in Class V in a nearby Bengali-medium girls' school. I have an elder brother who reads in a nearby boys' school in class VII.... I along with my elder brother take tuition in the morning and then go to school.... After I return from the school I play with my friends.... At the dusk I again prepare my lessons. Our mother keeps a strict vigil on our study....'

Thus one can conclude that access to primary education in the Control Group was far more severely restricted than in the

Programme Group. The author found that educating their children was a very low priority for the adults of the Control Group and they were more interested in sending their children out to work.

SECTION IV—CONDITION OF URBAN MARGINALITY AMONG THE STUDIED POPULATION

The author made a detailed study of the condition of urban marginality among these populations in details in terms of birth places, holding of ration card for public distribution system and voting status of the studied populations. The author also examined the condition of urban marginality of the studied populations with the presence or absence of some indicators on the collective consumption[21] available to the studied population.

The distribution of these people *according to the place of birth* (Table 3.10.8) of these people indicates that in All Populations most of these people were either born in Kolkata (36.94 per cent), or Bangladesh (24.19 per cent). 10.31 per cent of the inhabitants were born in the adjoining districts of West Bengal while migrants from Bihar and Jharkhand constituted 20.45 per cent of the population. 2.11 per cent of the respondents gave Uttar Pradesh as their place of birth. 3.80 per cent of the inhabitants came from states other than UP, Bihar or Jharkhand while only 2.07 per cent came from the other districts of West Bengal. The high frequency of the place of birth in the city of Kolkata among these people indicates that these settlements were established long ago and many of the respondents have lived there for a long time. At the same time, the high frequencies of Bangladesh and Bihar-Jharkhand as the places of birth would mean that these settlements were still accommodating trickle of new migrants not only from outside the state but also from the neighbouring country Bangladesh during the time of this fieldwork. In the Control Group most people (28.52 per cent) were born in Bangladesh, followed by Bihar and Jharkhand[22] (26.45 per cent) and Kolkata (24.97 per cent). In the Programme Group, on the other hand, highest incidences (73.66 per cent) of persons had Kolkata as the place of birth followed by the adjoining districts of West Bengal (12.13 per cent) and Bangladesh (11.03 per cent). These statistics in the Programme Group showed that this settlement became progressively closed for the migrants from outside the state or country. Those people who were born elsewhere in West Bengal or Bangladesh were mostly the elderly people who migrated to this settlement long ago.

In the city of Kolkata, like many other Indian cities, *holding of ration card* for public distribution system (Table 3.10.9) by an individual and/or a family validates the status of said individual and/or family as legal inhabitants of the city. Possession of ration card in the city of Kolkata would also mean access to some of the subsidised food-items and Kerosene oil. The author studied the frequency of holding of this ration card in All Populations where it was found that only 18.18 per cent hold ration cards. The reason for such a low frequency of ration card holding was the virtual absence of ration cards in the Control Group. To obtain a ration card in the city of Kolkata one needs to have a valid and a permanent residential address. This was an impossible proposition for the inhabitants of Population-I and Population-II, as these settlements were not legalised by the authorities (urban or municipal). Thus the distribution of the Control Group according to holding of ration card of PDS or public distribution system showed that a very negligible proportion (0.54 per cent) possessed ration card in these two settlements. Those possessing ration cards in the Control Group could not record their dwelling places as their addresses. On the contrary, all of the persons possessing ration cards recorded the addresses of their workplaces as their residences. This distribution in the Programme Group, which was a legalised settlement, showed a completely different picture in this regard where as high as 72.27 per cent of the population possesses ration card. According to the local parameter, this high incidence of possession of ration card would also reflect that the people in the Programme Group were regarded as the legal inhabitants of the city of Kolkata by the authorities.

Another related indicator on the legitimacy of the urban citizenship is the distribution *according to the voting status* (Table 3.10.10) which the author studied among these people.

This distribution showed that most of the possible voters (46.78 per cent of the total populations) were registered as legitimate voters (39.49 per cent). Contrary to the popular notion that the voting status makes a person a legal inhabitant of the city, it was observed from the distribution according to the status as a voter in the Control Group that as high as 32.84 per cent (where the proportion of possible voter was 41.07 per cent of the total population) of these people had their names in the electoral roll. However, many of the possible voters could not enter their names in the electoral roll.

> **Case Study No. 8 (Population-I):** 'My name is Momena Begum...aged about 35 years. I am living in this settlement for the last twenty years.... We, i.e. my husband and I, have names in the voters' list.... A local political leader has registered our names after we settled here.... No, we do not have any ration card.... We buy rice and kerosene from the (open) market with much higher price.... But we have names in the voters' list for the last twenty years.... They promised us to protect during the time of crisis.... We always cast our votes according to the wish of the local leaders.... Now when the information of the demolition of our settlement came to us, we went to those leaders.... But they are saying that it is inevitable.... The road has to be widened.... We went to our local councillor.... The councillor also repeated the same.... Where shall we go after that, we just do not know.... We left our home in Bangladesh long ago....'

The same distribution in the Programme Group, on the other hand, reflects an expected trend where most (59.86 per cent) of the possible voters (64.27 per cent of the total population) found their names in the electoral roll. This trend further confirms the legitimate status of the Population-III in the city of Kolkata.

> **Case Study No. 9 (Population-III):** 'I am Santosh Manna; my age is 42 years.... I am living in this settlement for the last twenty-five years.... Originally I am from Medinipore.... When I settled here I applied

for my family's ration card through some locally influential people and I got those ration cards.... It came as a great help for me during that time of crisis.... At one point of time the ration card was the only essential document for identification in various stages of our life like admitting my son in the school, applying for different available subsidies, registering my son's name in the employment exchange.... After I received the ration card I got my name registered in the electoral roll during early 1980s.... Now they have also given a photo-identity card, it is a very helpful gesture on behalf of the government....'

The author also studied the distribution of households among these people *according to the presence of some indicators on collective consumption* (Table 3.10.11). This distribution reveals the state of collective consumption in all the studied settlements. Thus all the households in All Populations meaning households in both the Control Group as well as the Programme Group got the facility of presence of at least one accessible primary school within 1 km. Only 28 per cent of the households in All Populations were enjoying the facility of an accessible hospital/health centre, playground and community centre within 1 km of the individual settlement. On a closer look it was found that none of the households in the Control Group had these facilities within 1 km but all the households in the Programme Group had all these facilities within 1 km. All the households in All Populations which means all the households in the Control Group as well as in the Programme Group were with the presence of motorable road in the vicinity of their settlements. Only 28 per cent of the households in All Populations had *pucca* arterial road within the settlement. None of the households in the Control Group were enjoying the facility of having *pucca* arterial road within the settlement but all the households in the Programme Group were having this facility. Similarly 28 per cent of the households in All Populations were enjoying the facility of garbage disposal system and planned drainage system in their settlements meaning the Control Group did not have any of these facilities whereas all the households in the

Programme Group were enjoying both of these facilities. If one observes the distribution of the population according to the facility of legally possessed electricity then it would be revealed that in All Populations only 30.13 per cent were with this facility. Settlement-wise distribution showed that in the Control Group none of the households had the legally obtained electricity while all the electrified households (98.09 per cent) in the Programme Group had obtained their electricity legally. Separate ventilation in the households was present in All Population in a very low frequency (26.80 per cent). Only 3.89 per cent of the households in the Control Group had separate ventilation while as high as 85.71 per cent of the households in the Programme Group were enjoying this facility. Very few households (8.13 per cent) were found to have separate family bathrooms in All Populations. While none of the households in the Control Group had this facility, compared to 29.05 per cent of households in the Programme Group had this facility. Only 20 per cent households in All Populations were with separate kitchens. Very few households (2.59 per cent) in the Control Group had separate kitchens while majority of the households (64.76 per cent) in the Programme Group were with separate kitchens. Water impermeable roofs and walls of the house ought to be regarded as one of the basic facilities in a rain-prone city like Kolkata. Only 41.20 per cent houses had water impermeable roofs and 57.20 per cent were with water impermeable walls in All Populations. Settlement-wise distribution showed that the majority of the households in the Control Group had water permeable roofs (66.30 per cent) and water permeable walls (56.85 per cent). In the Programme Group the frequency of occurrence of water permeable roofs was rather low (39.52 per cent) and that of water permeable walls was even lower (6.67 per cent). It was also seen during this fieldwork that almost half of the households (49.47 per cent) in All Populations had to endure waterlogging of floor during rainy seasons. While majority of the households (64.41 per cent) in the Control Group had to cope with waterlogging on the floor especially during the rainy season, the Programme Group fared much better with only 3.33 per cent of the households facing this problem. Lastly, only 2.80 per cent households in All Populations were with own household taps as the source of drinking water as none of the households in the Control Group had its own tap as a source of drinking water and very few households (10.00 per cent) in the Programme Group were with this facility. These frequency distributions have further reiterated our general observation that the availability of collective consumption was much meagre among the households in Control Group compared those in the Programme Group.

Thus the Control Group population lacked integration with the urban life as far as birth places, presence of property at the native places, time of settlement, holding of ration card for public distribution system, voting status and the presence of some indicators on the collective consumption are concerned. The author also found during his fieldwork that the Programme Group people were much more integrated with the urban life of Kolkata in all these aspects, a reflection on the differences in the level of urban marginality between the two groups of populations.

SECTION V—ECONOMIC CONDITION OF THE POPULATIONS

After the study on the aspects of marginalisation of these populations, the author explored the economic condition of the families of the populations to obtain an idea on the economic background of the families of Control Group and the Programme Group which might shed some light on the factors at the household level responsible for child labour.

Distribution of *persons in labour force*[23] *and persons actually working* (Table 3.10.12) revealed important patterns of the involvement of these people in work in all the three settlements. In this connection it must be mentioned here that the persons in the labour force or the labour force participation rate (LFPR) is the proportion of person in the age group 15 years and above who are either working (i.e. employed) on the usual principal and subsidiary status or seeking or available for work (i.e. presently unemployed). The author also took account of the persons (in the age group 15 and above) in actual work as this account along with that of the child labourers would be necessary to calculate the frequency of persons pursuing different kinds of occupations. It was found that 78.25 per cent of these people in All Populations were in the labour force and 74.91 per cent of the population in actual work which can considered as a very high occurrence when compared with the national or the state levels in combined areas as well as in the urban areas.[24] This labour force participation trend was more frequent among the males (91.33 per cent) than the females (65.46 per cent) both were higher than the national and state level figures in combined areas and in urban areas.[25] It was also evident from this distribution that in the Control Group, 90.82 per cent were in the labour force and 88.24 per cent of the population in actual work during the time of this study which was again more than the national or the state figures in combined areas as well as in the urban areas. This labour force participation trend was more frequent among the males (96.48 per cent) than the females (85.42 per cent) both of which were also higher than the national as well as the state level in combined areas and in urban areas. Accordingly persons in actual work varied in the Control Group where 88.24 per cent of the people were in actual work. At the same time 94.91 per cent males and 81.87 per cent females in the Control Group were in the labour force, both these percentages were slightly lower than the proportions of persons in the labour force. In the Programme Group, 53.89 per cent people were in the labour force which was slightly higher than the trends available in the national level and the state level in the urban areas but lower in comparison with the national and state figures in combined areas. 81.68 per cent of the men and 25.47 per cent of the females were in the labour force. All three figures were slightly higher than the national and the state levels in the urban areas but lower than the overall proportions in combined areas at the national and the state averages. In the Programme Group too, the proportion of persons in actual workforce was slightly lower than the persons in the labour force (49.07 per cent). Accordingly, 75.09 per cent males and 22.47 per cent females were actually employed both of which were again slightly lower than the respective proportions of males and females in the labour force.

The incidence of unemployment in India is defined as the percentage of persons unemployed in the age group 15 years and above on the usual principal and subsidiary status to the total number of persons in the labour force. The incidence of unemployment is not estimated in India by any sort of official employment registration system and/or unemployment registration system which create a huge gap between the official estimation and the reality on the ground. Thus the distribution of these people *according to the incidence of unemployment* (Table 3.10.13) must start with few notes. One, among these marginalised people especially in the Control Group, the majority of the population were engaged in some unstable and subsistence level incomes in the informal sector of the economy, also referred to as incidences of 'misemployment'. Two, in the Control Group a very high percentage of children were in actual workforce that could not be accounted for in the present estimates on the employment and unemployment. Three, the author observed that owing to their precarious financial circumstances the loss of earning on a single day could push individuals in the Control Group to the brink of starvation. Thus, they used to try to get engaged in every sort of work each day which could bring some money to them. All these three factors usually kept the estimated figures on unemployment to a much lower level than the actual figure as it did in these settlements (particularly in the Control Group) in this regard. Thus in All Populations, the total unemployment frequency was only 4.27 per cent. Among the males this frequency was 6.28 per cent and among the females it was 5.14 per cent. All these were surprisingly lower that the national and the state ratios in 1999–2000 in the combined areas as well as urban areas, according to NSSO 55th Round study.[26] It must be mentioned here that neither any of these unemployed nor any of those misemployed people was registered with the government employment exchange during the time of fieldwork. This distribution showed that in the Control Group, 2.79 per cent of the labour forces were unemployed. This trend was higher among the females (4.16 per cent) than the males (1.63 per cent) in the Control Group.

> **Case Study No. 10 (Population-II):** 'My name is Md. Eklakhi.... I am 19 years old.... I live in this settlement since my birth.... I am yet to get married.... I am single, currently working as a helper in construction work.... Earlier I used to work as a scrap-picker.... During the rainy season the job of scrap-picking does not bring much money and with rain-soaked body I often get ill.... During the winters also scrap-picking becomes almost punishing owing to the severe cold.... I look for alternative jobs during these seasons.... I do not have a fixed job.... I do whatever job is available to me at any point of time if I feel that job would bring money to me.... My father cannot feed the entire family.... If I cannot earn I, along with many of my family members, would have to starve.... I always look for a better job so desperately. I want to marry soon but I am apprehensive about what would I do if I do not get a suitable job by then....'

In the Programme Group, the incidence of unemployment was 8.93 per cent, 8.07 per cent of which were males and 11.76 per cent were females. All these figures were higher than the national and the state estimates. This was expected in the Programme Group as the incidences of misemployment were much lower than in the Control Group. The following is an example of registered unemployed found during this fieldwork.

> **Case Study No. 11 (Population-III):** 'My name is Shyamal Das; my age is 23 years...unmarried. I am living in this settlement since my birth.... I am an arts graduate from the University of Calcutta. I am presently looking for a job and I have registered my name in the employment exchange.... I know the job-market is very bad but I still wish to get a job preferably in a school as a school teacher.... I now give private tuitions to some school students but the amount I earn is too meagre to offset even my daily expenses.... Things are turning bad to worse in recent days as my father is on the verge of his retirement. I need to get a job within one and half years from now, failing which our family may face

immense difficulty as my father do not come in any pension scheme....'

The author also studied the distribution of children *according to the participation in labour force and actually working* (Table 3.10.14) among these people. In All Populations 74.69 per cent children (in the age groups 5-9 and 10-14 years) were in the labour force (76.65 per cent boys and 89.07 per cent girls). On the other hand, 72.02 per cent children were actually working during this fieldwork of which 72.61 per cent were boys and 71.36 per cent were girls. These figures are phenomenally high when compared with the national and the state estimates of child labourers in 1991 in combined areas[27] as well as in urban areas.[28] In the Control Group, 89.86 per cent children (in the age groups 5-9 and 10-14 years) were in the labour force. Gender-wise break up showed in the Control Group that 90.59 per cent boys and 89.07 per cent girls were in the labour force. In the Control Group, 84.19 per cent of the children were actually working. Again the gender-wise distribution showed that 86.01 per cent boys and 82.24 per cent girls were actually working. On a closer study of this distribution it was found that this trend of high preponderance of child labourers was slightly more prominent in Population-II (where 84.40 per cent children were found working) than Population-I (where 83.97 per cent children were working). In fact Population-I had higher potential child labour in the form of children in the labour force (89.95 per cent). All the necessary elaborations regarding child labour have been made in later part of this section where the author will specifically deal with the problem of child labour. However, for the present purpose, it could be said in accordance to the findings that during the time of study of the Population-I it was on the verge of getting evicted and the parents faced with the eventuality about the future of their families may have discontinued the study of some of their children. Thus they made their children available in the labour force. In the Programme Group, 5.80 per cent children were in the labour force (6.41 per cent males and 5.00 per cent females). It has been seen from the same distribution that 5.07 per cent children were working in the Programme Group.

Gender-wise break-up showed that in the Programme Group, 5.13 per cent boys and 5.00 per cent girls were actually working. All these figures are nearer to the national and the state estimates on child labourers in 1991 in the combined areas as well as in the urban areas.

The author found that the estimates of the *working children and the working adults of these populations* (Table 3.10.15) can give an idea about the contrasting involvement in workforce. In All Populations, 35.22 per cent of the working population were children. Frequency distribution according to gender showed that 33.14 per cent of the working males were children and a higher 37.90 per cent of the working females were children. On a closer look, one can find that in the Control Group, 40.91 per cent of the workforce was composed of child labourers in comparison with 59.09 per cent working adults. Gender-wise divisions would indicate that in the Control Group 41.07 per cent of the male workers were children and 58.93 per cent were adults. On the other hand, 40.73 per cent of the female workers were children and 59.27 per cent were adults in this Control Group. The high tendency of child labourers in the working force was more marked in Population-I where 60.59 per cent workers were children. Here children constituted 61.09 per cent of male workers and 60.00 per cent of female workers. This distribution in the Programme Group reflected a completely different picture with only 2.57 per cent of the workers being children. Only 1.91 per cent of the male workforce were children and a slightly higher i.e. 4.76 per cent proportion of females were working children. Negligible involvement of the children in workforce was a feature of the Programme Group.

The distribution of these populations *according to the types of primary occupation* (Table 3.10.16) showed that in All Populations only 6.60 per cent (with an overwhelming male majority) were salaried workers in the traditional sector of economy (Type-A) followed by skilled workers (*mistris*), handicraft persons and small merchants (12.60 per cent). The fieldwork also showed that in All Populations as high as 44.98 per cent were urban waste recycle workers (Type-E) and 35.00 per cent were the sellers of their labour to people for the personal service and consumption of the buyers instead of using their labour power to obtain a surplus value (Type-C). It would, however, be important to note that the skin sellers exchanging their survival against the possibility of potential destruction (e.g. prostitute, delinquent, etc.) or trading their deterioration (e.g. beggar) (Type-D), which is a common finding among the marginalised population throughout the Third World, were barely among these people. Only a few beggars (0.43 per cent) were found in the Type-D occupation and all of them were found in the Control Group. One could also see that in All Populations men were more heavily represented than women in the Type-B occupation (of skilled workers, etc.) (9.76 per cent to 2.84 per cent). A similar pattern was witnessed in Type-E occupation (i.e. the urban waste recycle work) (23.50 per cent to 21.48 per cent) in All Populations. On the other hand, Type-C occupations (i.e. sellers of their labour, etc.) were more common among the females (18.32 per cent) than the males (16.68 per cent). A break up of the populations in the Control Group according to occupational categories shows that 1.28 per cent of the total population was involved in Type-A occupations, 9.22 per cent in Type-B occupations, 52.75 per cent were urban waste recycle workers i.e. Type-E occupation and 36.24 per cent were pursuing Type-C occupations. On a closer look at this distribution it might be said that this trend of preponderance of Type-E and Type-C primary occupations, which mostly brings about the subsistence level wage, was more prominent in Population-II among these two populations. Only 0.51 per cent of the Population-I was involved in Type-D occupations. The author, on further investigation, found that there were few cases of incomes from prostitution as well as delinquency in the Control Group but neither prostitution nor delinquency was the primary occupation for any of the inhabitants in the Control Group. These differences in the frequencies of the types of the primary occupations between the Control Group and the Programme Group also showed that the people in the Programme Group had more stable sources of income in comparison to the Control Group. *Gender-wise break-up* of this frequency distribution in the Control Group showed that Type-B occupations were more frequent among the males (6.59 per cent) than the females (2.62 per cent). Males were slightly more represented than females in Type-E occupations (27.53 per cent to 25.22 per cent) while females were more heavily represented in Type-C occupations (19.14 per cent to 17.09 per cent). The Programme Group showed a different picture altogether. A high proportion of people were engaged in Type-A occupations in traditional sector (37.13 per cent) and another substantial proportion of population (31.99 per cent) were engaged in Type-B occupations. Both of these occupations were stable and had higher earning potential. The frequency of people engaged in Type-C occupations, which was the only mentionable category with substantive level of wages in the Programme Group, was also high (27.94 per cent). It must also be mentioned here that in conformity with the general trend of very low frequency of the working females in the Programme Group. It was also seen that the frequencies of females engaged in the better occupations in the Programme Group were in lesser proportions. But more than half of the females (i.e. 13.60 per cent of the total working population in the Programme Group) were engaged in Type-C occupations.

Consistent with the earlier findings on occupations, the distribution of the households among these people *according to the family income per day* (Table 3.10.17) indicated that in All Populations most of the households were earning between Rs. 51 to Rs. 75 per day during the time of this fieldwork, followed by the households earning less than Rs. 50 or less per day (18.00 per cent). Both these frequencies indicate that their incomes were below the subsistence level and most of these families did not have any security of work. Thus most of these families would slip below the poverty line[29] when compared with national and state data in the urban areas.[30] It must also be mentioned here that during this fieldwork a sizeable proportion (29.73 per cent) of the households in All Populations were found to be earning more than Rs. 100 per day (overwhelming proportion of these households came from the Programme Group). In the Control Group it was also evident that most of the households earned between Rs. 51 to Rs. 75 per day (49.63 per cent). Households earning Rs. 50 or less per day were also in high frequency (23.15 per cent) in the Control Group. Household incomes between Rs. 76 to Rs. 100 (16.30 per cent) and above Rs. 100 per day (10.93 per cent) were in lower frequencies in the Control Group which would indicate their poor economic condition overall. In the Programme Group, on the other hand, overwhelming proportion of households (76.43 per cent) were found to have incomes over Rs. 100 per day during the fieldwork and the frequency of households with an income between Rs. 76 to Rs. 100 per day came next (16.91 per cent). There were few households which were earning Rs. 50 or less per day (3.68 per cent) and between Rs. 51 and Rs. 75 per day (6.99 per cent). These facts would indicate that in the Programme Group most of the people were in better condition than the Control Group.

The distribution of the households in these populations *according to the level of monthly savings* (Table 3.10.18) showed that in nearly half of the households in All Populations (48.53 per cent) monthly savings were non-existent and as high as 18.93 per cent of the households could only save less than Rs. 100 per month. These trends were consistent with their income as most of them earn very meagre amount throughout the year. Households in All Populations saving more than Rs. 200 per month (16.67 per cent) and between Rs. 101 to Rs. 200 per month (15.87 per cent) were also present in higher frequencies (though majority of these households come from the Programme Group). In the Control Group most (61.11 per cent) of the families did not have any monthly savings and few had monthly savings of less than Rs. 100 (17.22 per cent) or between Rs. 101 and Rs. 200 (12.22 per cent) and fewer households (8.52 per cent) were found to have a monthly savings of more than Rs. 200. This trend was in conformity with the overall economic condition of the Control Group. The households in the Programme Group were in better state in terms of monthly savings. Thus more households in the Programme Group had monthly savings of more than Rs. 200 (35.24 per cent) and between Rs. 101 and Rs. 200 (25.24 per cent). Households with no monthly savings and little monthly savings of less than Rs. 100 were also found in mentionable frequencies of 16.19 per cent and 23.33 per cent respectively in the Programme Group.

From the study of the economic profile of the populations reveals that the Control Group populations were in a precarious economic condition with meagre as well as unsecured income and very few or non-existent savings. The Programme Group, on the other hand, had more secured income with better returns and the people living in that settlement had few savings which serve as an essential cushion against the regular and unforeseen expenditures. The author will later explore this discursive space, whether this vulnerability has led to the proliferation of child labour problem in the Control Group.

SECTION VI—POPULATION AND EDUCATIONAL PROFILES OF THE CHILD LABOURERS

Thus the above observations on the inhabitants of the Control Group and the Programme Group on population profile, educational aspects, integration with the urban life and economic condition showed that the Control Group people were in a more precarious existence than the Programme Group people. In the next few sections of this chapter the author would study whether this condition of the Control Group was associated with the creation and/or prevalence of child labour in that population.

Distribution of the child labourers *according to the age and sex* (Table 3.10.19) showed that in All Populations child labourers from the age group 10-14 years (51.64 per cent) was slightly higher in frequency than the child labourers from the age group 5-9 years (48.46 per cent). Similarly female child labourers (47.06 per cent) were a little less frequent than the male child labourers (52.94 per cent). This feature was prevalent among both the age groups i.e. 5-9 years and 10-14 years. Also in the Control Group a majority of the child labourers came from the age group 10-14 years (51.02 per cent) compared to the other age group i.e. 5-9 years (48.98 per cent). A closer study of this distribution, however, showed that in

Population-II the frequency of child labourers in the age group 5-9 years was higher (53.94 per cent) than in the age group 10-14 years (46.06 per cent). It could also be seen that in the Control Group, the frequency of boys among the child labourers was higher (52.90 per cent) than the girls (47.10 per cent). The preponderance of the boys among the child labourers was visible in both the age groups of 5-9 years and 10-14 years. In the Programme Group no child labourer was found in the age group 5-9 years and all the child labours (0.97 per cent of the total population i.e. only seven children) came in the age group 10-14 years. The frequency of boys (57.14 per cent) among the child labourers was higher than girls (42.86 per cent) here.[31]

Similar picture emerges when we see the distribution of *child labourers and the child populations according to age and sex* (Table 3.10.20). This distribution showed that in All Populations as high as 67.75 per cent of the children in the age group 5-9 years were child labourers during this fieldwork; at the same time 69.79 per cent of the boys and 65.64 per cent of the girls in this age group were child labourers. It must be mentioned here that all these child labourers in the age group 5-9 years came from the Control Group. In the age group 10-14 years child labourers in All Populations were in an even higher frequency (76.55 per cent) both among the boys (75.42 per cent) and the girls (77.89 per cent). Again one would find that the overwhelming proportion of these child labourers were from the Control Group. In the Control Group, quite predictably 78.25 per cent of the children in the age group 5-9 years were child labourers and an even higher percentage of the children (90.81 per cent) in the age group 10-14 years were child labourers. In both cases the frequency of child labourers was weighted towards the boys. Thus 80.39 per cent of the boys in the age group 5-9 years were child labourers in the Control Group compared to 76.02 per cent girls in the same age group. On the other hand, 92.06 per cent of the boys in the age group 10-14 years were child labourers in the Control Group in comparison to 89.41 per cent of the girls of the similar age group. This is sharp contrast to the picture in the Programme Group where no child labourer was found in the age group

5-9 years and only 9.21 per cent of the children in the age group 10-14 years were found to be working. Though it was seen from the distribution that 8.51 per cent of the boys and 10.34 per cent of the girls were child labourers these figures have to be viewed in the backdrop of an overall low frequency of children in that age group. Both the last two distributions would demonstrate the desperation among these people, which had driven the parents to release their children to the labour market at a tender age, as found among the people in the Control Group. The Programme Group, on the other hand, was much more cushioned from this desperation and the phenomenon of child labour was almost non-existent.

Distribution of the *child labourers according to the standard of education* (Table 3.10.21) revealed that more than half of the child labourers (56.81 per cent) were non-literates and another sizable proportion (22.44 per cent) could sign their names only. This lack of literacy was more prominent among the girl child labourers (43.34 per cent) than their male counterpart (13.47 per cent). Most of the other child labourers read up to the classes between I to IV (15.79 per cent) and most of them were boys (12.69 per cent). Few child labourers (4.95 per cent) read up to the class V or above standard and all these child labourers were boys. Quite expectedly, in the Control Group majority of the child labourers were non-literates (57.43 per cent) or could sign their names only (22.69 per cent). Taken together, these categories are coterminous with the absence of effective literacy. However, many of these child labourers (15.34 per cent) in the Control Group either read up to or were still reading in the classes between I to IV and in the classes between V and above (4.54 per cent) during the time of this fieldwork. On the other hand, all the child labourers in the Programme Group were literates and most of the male child labourers were still continuing their study during the time of this fieldwork. This different trend in the Programme Group could not change the overall trends of the child labourers in all the three populations. Thus the trends in the Control Group would epitomize the overall standard of education among the child labourers which was affected by the presence of an overwhelming majority of child labourers in the Control Group.

Similarly the distribution of child labourers according to the years of schooling (Table 3.10.22) confirmed that most of the child labourers in All Populations either never went to the school (56.81 per cent) or spend very little time i.e. one year to three years (32.20 per cent) in school. Few child labourers (10.99 per cent), nevertheless, spent or were spending more than three years in school during this fieldwork. In the Control Group there were as many as 57.43 per cent of child labourers had never crossed the threshold of a school which would indicate a very low level of interest among the parents to send their children to the school. Others either spent up to three years in school (31.92 per cent) or more than three years in school (10.64 per cent). On the other hand, in the Programme Group every child labourer went to school either for one to five years (57.14 per cent) or for more than five years (42.86 per cent). This trend, however, could not change the overall dismal trend of school going among the child labourers.

If we continue our observations on the different aspects of education among these child labourers we would find that the distribution of *child labourers according to the continuity of study* (Table 3.10.23) reflected that as high as 54.48 per cent of the child labourers in All Populations had already discontinued their studies. This trend was particularly visible among the child labourers in the Control Group where 54.78 per cent of the child labourers discontinued study whereas 42.86 per cent (numbering only three) in the Programme Group were had similar fate. This was considered as an indicative of high drop-out rate[32] and which was in conformity with the national and state trend.[33] It was also observed from this distribution that only 7.53 per cent of these child labourers were continuing their study in formal schools during the time of this fieldwork. This trend was even lower in the Control Group (6.25 per cent) but much higher in the Programme Group (57.14 per cent). On the other hand, majority (37.99 per cent) of the child labourers who were continuing their study during the fieldwork were reading in the non-formal schools run by some NGOs. This trend of reading in non-formal schools was only found in the Control Group.

If the distribution of the *non-literate or dropped out child labourers according to the main reason for leaving or not sending to school* (Table 3.10.24) are studied then it would further be revealed that in majority of the cases in All Populations the responses came in favour of the families' need of the children's contribution (38.87 per cent) followed by the inability of the respective families to afford the study (37.76 per cent). In 18.89 per cent cases the children needed money for their own survival as the family could not support them. Other such reasons included uninterested in study (5.01 per cent) and investing time to learn something meaningful in the apprenticeship of some skilled job (3.66 per cent). In the Control Group this trend was almost identical where most frequently the responses came in favour of the families' inability to continue the study (37.76 per cent) or the families' need of the children's contribution (34.87 per cent). This trend was however not so much visible in the Programme Group where in most of the cases the main reason for leaving or not sending to school was the shifting of interest to the apprenticeship to a skilled job (66.67 per cent). But again this trend in the Programme Group could hardly alter the overall trend in this regard among the child labourers.

Thus the population and educational profiles of the child labourers indicate that almost all of the child labourers were from the Control Group. Most of the children (except from the age group of 0-5 years of age) in the Control Group are child labourers. Most of these child labourers were either deprived of school education or somehow managing to cling on the non-formal school, though irregularly. This trend gives us an idea of condition of child labourers especially in the Control Group. Programme Group had managed to become almost free from the problem of child labour.

SECTION VII—ECONOMIC PROFILE OF THE CHILD LABOURERS

As the population and educational profile of child labour indicate, in the studied populations child labourers were eking out their subsistence in various ways which will be revealed when we study the economic profile of this child labour population.

The author observed the distribution of the *child labour population according to the status as a labourer* (Table 3.10.25). It showed that overwhelming proportions of the child labourers in All Populations were wage earners (80.65 per cent) followed by the household businesses/occupations (11.30 per cent) or self-employed (8.05 per cent). In the Control Group this trend was quite similar with 81.22 per cent of the child labourer being wage-earners, 10.80 per cent involved in household businesses/occupations and 7.98 per cent self-employed. In the Programme Group, however, a majority of the child labourers were in household businesses/occupations (57.14 per cent). The girls were more frequently employed in household businesses/occupations (7.59 per cent) in comparison to their male counterpart (3.72 per cent). Thus the girls, apart from in their own household occupations/businesses, were more likely to be employed in the other occupations which engage them in the households like domestic helps.

Observations on the distribution of the *child labourers according to the age of entering work* (Table 3.10.26) are very important for the present context. This distribution showed that most of the child labourers in All Populations entered in work between the ages of 6 years and 9 years (41.02 per cent). The next frequent group in which child labourers entered work was between the ages of 10 years and 14 years (39.01 per cent). The other notable fact which emerged from this distribution was that a large section of these child labourers entered in work at the tender age of below 6 years (19.97 per cent). This trend was even been more visible among the girls (11.45 per cent) than the boys (8.51 per cent). This trend of large absorption of children in the workforce on or before the school enrolment year (i.e. 6 years) was also substantiated by the very high frequency of non-literates among these children especially among the girls. Similar trends were also visible among the child labourers in the Control Group where 41.16 per cent entered in the work between the ages of 6 years and 9 years, 38.65 per cent between 10 years and 14 years and another 20.19 per cent entered below the age of 6 years. However, in the Programme Group no child entered the workforce at the age of below 6 years and most of them entered between the ages of 10 years and 14 years.

Working hour-wise distribution of these child labourers (Table 3.10.27) showed that for the majority of the child labourers in All Populations, the working hours were over 6 hours per day (74.77 per cent). For about a quarter of the total population studied these working hours ranged from 2 hours to 6 hours (14.09 per cent) or less than 2 hours (11.14 per cent). Similar trend was also visible among the child labourers in the Control Group where 75.27 per cent were working above 6 hours per day, 13.46 per cent between 2 hours and 6 hours per day and 11.11 per cent less than 2 hours per day. In the Programme Group only one boy (14.29 per cent) was working above 6 hours per day while most of the child labourers here generally used to work between 2 hours and 6 hours (71.43 per cent). But again this lower incidence of longer working hours in the Programme Group had no impact on the overall trends on working hours among the child labourers.

The author also studied the distribution of the *child labourers according to the availability of resting time within the working hours* (Table 3.10.28). It showed that 60.53 per cent of the child labourers in All Populations were allowed to have a resting time of less than 30 minutes within their working hours. But a more noticeable fact was that as high as 36.69 per cent of these children were not allowed to have any rest during their working hours. There were, however, some child labourers who used to get a resting time between 30 minutes and one hour (2.79 per cent). But none of them were getting a resting time of more than one hour. In the Control Group, the above trend was almost identical with 61.03 per cent of the child labourers were getting less than 30 minutes of resting time and 37.09 per cent of them were working without any resting time. However, in the Programme Group most of the child labourers (85.71 per cent) were granted a resting time ranging from 30 minutes to one hour.

If we look at the distribution of the *child labourers according to the number of working days in a week*[34] (Table 3.10.29) then most of the child labourers in All Populations were working 6 days a week (59.60 per cent) and a very high proportion of them were working in all the 7 days in a week (32.30 per cent). Other categories like working for 5 days (2.79 per cent), 4 days (2.01 per cent), 3 days (1.39 per cent) or less than 3 days in a week (2.01 per cent) occurred in much lesser frequencies among them. Similar trend was visible among the child labourers of the Control Group where 59.62 per cent child labourers were working in 6 days a week and 32.08 per cent worked in all the 7 days in a week. In the Programme Group this trend was also visible where 42.86 per cent were working in all the 7 days in a week and 57.14 per cent were working in 6 days a week. But it must be mentioned here that in the Programme Group all the child labourers were working in all the 7 days in a week (one boy and two girls in particular), were working in their domestic units where the pressure of work was much lower.

The distribution of the *child labourers according to the type of sector (formal/informal) of economy* (Table 3.10.30) reveals that as high as 98.02 per cent of the child labourers in All Populations were working in the informal sector of economy. The tiny majority of child labourers (1.08 per cent) who were absorbed in the formal sector of the economy were denied any formal appointment and were mostly engaged in some badly paid low skill jobs in those establishments. This trend was again consistent with that in the Control Group where 99.06 per cent of the child labourers were employed in the informal sector. In the Programme Group the proportion of child labourers in the informal sector was little lower (85.71 per cent) and correspondingly the proportion of child labourers in the formal sector was higher (14.29 per cent).

Distribution of the *child labourers according to the type of occupation* (Table 3.10.31) showed that most of these child labourers in All Populations were either engaged as urban waste recycle workers i.e. Type-E occupation (42.72 per cent) or in occupations which the author termed as the sellers of their labour to people for the personal service and consumption of the buyers instead of using their labour power to obtain a surplus value i.e. Type-C occupations (42.57 per cent). Some of these children were also engaged as apprentices to skilled workers or handicraft persons or small merchants i.e. Type-B (13.47 per cent) and few were in the 'traditional' or formal sector of economy i.e. Type-A (1.08 per cent) though as temporary workers as well as in the occupations which the author called as skin sellers exchanging their survival against the possibility of potential destruction or deterioration i.e. Type-D occupations (0.31 per cent). Gender-wise frequency distribution showed that the male child labourers were more concentrated in the Type-E and Type-B occupations. On the other hand, female child labourers were more frequently employed in Type-C occupations. In the Control Group the trend regarding the type of primary occupation remained the same where 43.19 per cent of the child labourers were in Type-E occupations, 42.57 per cent in Type-C occupations, 13.15 per cent in Type-B occupations, 0.94 per cent in Type-A occupations and 0.31 per cent in Type-D occupations. Gender-wise distribution again showed almost identical features among the child labourers in All Populations. In the Programme Group this trend was quite different where the child labourers were engaged in Type-B occupations (42.86 per cent), Type-C occupations (42.86 per cent) and Type-A occupations (14.29 per cent). None of these child labourers in the Programme Group were engaged in Type-D and Type-E occupations. No female child labourer in the Programme Group was found Type-A occupations and a smaller proportion of female child labourers were found in Type-B occupations while in Type-C occupations female child labourers were found more frequently.

When these primary occupations were actually broken *according to the details of the individual occupations* (Table 3.10.32) then they corroborated the earlier findings on primary occupations. Most frequently found occupational type of these child labourers was Type-E. From the frequencies of occupations within Type-E category one can find that scrap pickers (30.34 per cent) was much higher than the other occupations in this type like the scrap sorters (7.28 per cent) and the door-to-door scrap buyers (5.11 per cent). Male child labourers were engaged more frequently in Type-E occupations i.e. as scrap pickers (14.86 per cent), door to door scrap buyers (4.18 per cent) or scrap sorters (4.02 per cent). In the category with the next highest concentration of child labourers i.e. Type-C occupations as high as 21.21 per cent were engaged as domestic helps (all of them were girls) and 7.12 per cent were tea stall/restaurant workers (majority of them were boys). Rest of the child labourers in this category were working as the helpers in construction works (2.94 per cent), porters (2.63 per cent), van/rickshaw pullers (2.32 per cent), *bidi* (flavoured Indian cigarette wrapped in tendu leaf) workers (2.32 per cent), shoe-shiners (2.01 per cent), *thonga* (paper-packet) makers (0.62 per cent) and a few miscellaneous occupations not falling in the earlier types (1.39 per cent). All the child labourers working as porters and van/rickshaw pullers were male child labourers but girls and boys were represented in almost equal proportions among the helpers in construction work. Boys dominated the category of *bidi* workers (1.39 per cent) whereas the girls were more frequently found among the shoe-shiners (1.08 per cent) and all the thonga-maker child labourers were girls. In the Type-B occupations most of the child labourers were apprentices to skilled workers or handicraft persons (12.69 per cent) and boys were in an overwhelming majority among these apprentices (11.61 per cent). A few of the Types-B child labourers were small merchants like fruit sellers, candy sellers, etc. (0.77 per cent) and all of them were boys. All the child labourers in Type-A occupations who were engaged as temporary workers without any formal contract (1.08 per cent) were boys. In the Control Group the author found the similar trend of Type-E occupations among the child labourers with 30.67 per cent were scrap pickers, 7.36 per cent scrap sorters and 5.33 per cent door-to-door scrap buyers (5.33 per cent). Type-C occupations found among these child labourers include 21.44 per cent domestic helps, 7.04 per cent tea stall/restaurant workers, 2.97 per cent helpers in construction, 2.66 per cent porters, 2.35 per cent van/rickshaw pullers, 2.35 per cent *bidi* workers, 2.03 per cent shoe-shiners, 0.31 per cent thonga makers and 1.41 per cent were engaged in other occupations. Gender-wise distribution of the child labourers in these occupations was also almost identical with the distribution of the child labourer in All Populations. The Programme Group, as indicated earlier, offered a rather different picture as none of the child labourers were engaged in the Type-D and Type-E occupations. In the Type-C occupations 28.57 per cent child labourers in the Programme Group were thonga makers (all were girls) and 14.29 per cent child labourers were tea stall/ restaurant workers (with only one child labour in this category being a boy). In Type-B occupations 28.57 per cent child labourers (male and female child labourers of equal proportion) were apprentices to skilled workers/handicraft persons and 14.29 per cent (i.e. one child labourer) was male small merchant. The Type-A occupation only consisted of one temporary worker in the traditional sector of economy (14.29 per cent).

The distribution of *child labourer according to the nature of work* (Table 3.10.33) reveals that as high as 23.37 per cent of the child labourers in All Populations were employed in the types of occupations, services and industries which were declared prohibited under the Child Labour (Prohibition and Regulation) Act, 1986. This trend of employing the children in the hazardous occupations, services and industries was only found in the Control Group where 23.63 per cent child labourers were in hazardous jobs. On the other hand, none of the child labourers in the Programme Group was in hazardous occupations, services and industries.

Distribution of the *child labourers according to the level of daily income*[35] (Table 3.10.34) showed that the daily income of most of the child labourers in All Populations was more than Rs. 10 but less than Rs. 25 (38.70 per cent). Child labourers earning less than Rs. 10 (28.02 per cent) formed the second most frequent category in All Populations. The frequency of child labourers earning more than Rs. 25 but less than Rs. 50 was also high (25.85 per cent) in All Populations. Few of these child labourers in All Populations were earning more than Rs. 50 per day (7.43 per cent) which can be considered as threshold of a decent income among these marginalised people. Among the child labourers in the Control Group this trend on the level of daily income was almost identical with the slightly declined frequency of child labourers earning less than Rs. 10 per day (27.86 per cent). One striking feature of the child labourers in the Programme Group was a high frequency of earning less than Rs. 10 (42.86 per cent). It must be mentioned in this context that all these child labourers (one boy and two girls) in the Programme Group were employed in the low-income family enterprises and their contributions were very limited in those enterprises.

It was observed from the *distribution of the child labourers according to the distance to workplace* (Table 3.10.35) that the workplaces of most of the child labourers in All Populations were at a distance of more than one km but within five kms (61.45 per cent) followed by the workplaces at a distance of within one km (25.70 per cent). A sizable section of these child labourers were having the workplaces at more far-flung places i.e. at the distance of more than five kms (12.85 per cent). It was also evident from this distribution that the girl child labourers had to travel lesser distances to attend work than the boys. The trend on the distance of workplace was identical in the Control Group where most of the child labourers were compelled to travel between one km and five kms for work (61.66 per cent) while 25.35 per cent were travelling less than one km (25.35 per cent). 12.99 per cent of these child labourers had workplaces at a distance of more than five kms. However, in the Programme Group 57.14 per cent of the child labourers had workplaces within the distance of one km while 42.86 per cent had their workplaces between one km and five kms. Distribution of the child labourers *according to the mode of transport to the workplace* (Table 3.10.36) confirmed that in majority of the cases (45.97 per cent) child labourers in All Populations required some mode of transport but could not avail that due to the dearth of money necessary to meet the cost of transport. Many of these children were working within the walkable distances from their homes (31.89 per cent) and as indicated earlier, this tendency was more visible among the girls (20.74 per cent) than the boys (11.14 per cent). It might also be noted that 19.97 per cent of these children were going to their workplaces by bus and while 1.39 per cent resorted to ticketless travelling by train. Fewer child labourers were travelling by train by purchasing tickets (0.77 per cent). In the Control Group, this trend on the mode of transport to workplace was almost the same where majority (46.48 per cent) could not afford transport cost even though they required some kind of transport. In the Programme Group, however, child labourers were either working within the walkable distances from their homes (71.43 per cent) or going to their workplaces by bus (28.57 per cent). But again the negligible presence of child labourers in the Programme Group could not make much of an impact on the overall trend.

Distribution of the *child labourers according to the part of earning spent on transport to the workplace* (Table 3.10.37) showed that 77.87 per cent of the child labourers in All Populations were spending nothing on transport to reach their workplaces while 14.07 per cent were spending less than 10 per cent of their earning for this purpose. 5.73 per cent were spending an amount between 10 per cent to 25 per cent of their earnings and even fewer were spending more than 25 per cent on transport to their workplaces (1.70 per cent). Control Group had broadly similar trends with 77.93 per cent spending nothing in transport to their workplaces. The child labourers in the Programme Group were either not spending anything on transport to their workplaces (71.43 per cent) or were spending 10 per cent to 25 per cent of their earnings for this purpose (28.57 per cent).

A study on the distribution of the *child labourer population according to the time spent to travel to their workplaces* (Table 3.10.38) revealed that in most cases among the child labourers in All Populations the time taken to travel to their workplaces were either less than 30 minutes (55.57 per cent) or none/ nominal (25.70 per cent). Some of these child labourers were compelled to travel for a period between 30 minutes and one hour (17.65 per cent) to reach to their workplaces while a few of them (1.08 per cent) used to travel for more than one hour to reach their workplaces. Like in the earlier three distributions the girl child labourers had to spend lesser times for travel to their workplace than their male counterpart. Similar trend was witnessed in the Control Group where majority of the child labourers had to travel for less than 30 minutes to reach their workplaces (55.87 per cent). 25.20 per cent of the child labourers in the Control Group had also been spending none or nominal time in this regard. In the Programme Group, on the other hand, the child labourers either needed no/nominal time (71.43 per cent) or less than 30 minutes (28.57 per cent) to reach their workplaces. Significant proportion of the child labourers in the Programme Group who had to travel to their workplaces were boys.

The author also studied the distribution of the *child labourers according to the facilities available at the workplaces* (Table 3.10.39) which showed that none of the workplaces of the child labourers in All Populations was adequately equipped with standard hazard prevention mechanisms while in 8.51 per cent cases these mechanisms were inadequately present in spite of its requirement and in as many as 14.86 per cent cases hazard prevention mechanisms were required but not present. For 76.63 per cent of these child labourers the hazard prevention facilities were not actually required because of the nature of their work. In the Control Group the trend was almost identical with 8.61 per cent child labourers did not have adequate hazard prevention facilities and another 15.02 per cent did not have any hazard prevention mechanism even though they worked in different hazardous industries. On the other hand, none of the child labourers in the Programme Group was engaged in work in the hazardous industries thus did not require any hazard prevention mechanism. Among the child labourers in All Populations self protection measures in most of the times were absent (21.36 per cent) even when it was required, while in few cases (2.01 per cent) these self-protection measures were inadequately present. In 76.63 per cent cases these measures were not required as they were not working in hazardous conditions. In the Control Group this trend was almost identical as none of the workplaces had adequate self-protection measures and in 21.60 per cent of the cases these measures were completely absent while in 2.03 per cent of the cases the self-protection measures were present inadequately. In the Programme

Group, as indicated above, none of the child labourers were working in hazardous conditions and thus did not need any self-protection measure. As far as the presence of first aid facilities in the workplaces of the child labourers in All Populations was concerned, these facilities were completely absent in majority of the workplaces (91.18 per cent). Though in a majority of the three settlements the child labourers were not exposed to the hazardous conditions the complete absence of first aid facilities cannot be justified. It was also seen that in 8.82 per cent cases first aid facilities were inadequately present while in none of these workplaces first aid facilities were adequately present. In the Control Group this trend was almost similar with 65.10 per cent of these child labourers devoid of any first aid facilities in their workplaces and 8.45 per cent having inadequate first aid facilities in their workplaces. In no workplace could the first aid facilities be described as adequate. Presence of adequate toilet facilities in the workplaces was something that none of the child labourers in All Populations enjoyed but 34.83 per cent of the cases it was inadequately present while 65.17 per cent of these child labourers did not have access to any toilet facility in their workplaces. In the Control Group, similarly, 65.10 per cent child labourers did not have any toilet facility in their workplaces while 34.90 per cent of them had some kind of inadequately arranged toilet facilities and none of the child labourers had access to adequate toilet facilities in their workplaces. In the Programme Group it was also found that in 71.43 per cent cases toilet facilities were inadequately present and 28.57 per cent of the child labourers did not have any toilet facilities in their workplaces.

A study of the distribution of the *number of accidents happened to the working children in their working life* (Table 3.10.40), it was revealed that most of the child labourers in All Populations experienced different accidents two to five times in their working life (44.27 per cent) even when they were not in the hazardous jobs and as many as 9.44 per cent of these child labourers (almost all of them were working in hazardous conditions) faced accidents for more than five times in their working life. However, the author could not find a single case among these accidents which caused a permanent damage of any part of the body or organ among these child labourers. All these accidents were experienced by the child labourers in the Control Group and none by the child labourers in the Programme Group.

Distribution of the *wage earning child labourer according to the number of employees present in the working unit* (Table 3.10.41) showed that most of the child labourers in All Populations were either working in units with five to ten fellow employees (51.65 per cent) or in units having less than five fellow employees (36.35 per cent). But quite a few of them was working in the units having more than ten fellow employees (12.00 per cent). An almost identical trend was found in the Control Group where 51.65 per cent wage earning child labourers were working in the units with five to ten fellow employees, 36.30 per cent working in units with less than five fellow employees and 12.04 per cent working in units with more than ten fellow employees. In the Programme Group only two children were wage earners. One of them was working in a unit having less than five fellow employees while the other in a unit with five to ten fellow employees.

Distribution of the *wage earning child labourers according to the recipients of the wage* (Table 3.10.42) further showed that 40.87 per cent of the wage earning child labourers in All Populations received their own wages. In other cases the recipients included the parents mostly their fathers (in 20.52 per cent cases) or mothers (in 10.26 per cent) or other elder members of the family (22.09 per cent). In some cases (6.26 per cent), some other people like relatives or neighbours received the wages of the working children. In the Control Group the trend was again almost identical with 40.66 per cent of the wage earning children receiving their own wages. The author found that the parents received wages for their children in 26.19 per cent cases (fathers in 20.59 per cent and mothers in 5.60 per cent of the cases) and for 22.16 per cent wage earning children the wages received by other elder member of the family while in 6.28 per cent of the cases the wages received by other relatives or neighbours of the children. In the Programme Group all the wage earning children were receiving their wages by themselves.

The distribution of the *fellow adult employees' behaviour in workplaces* (Table 3.10.43) showed that most of the wage earning children in All Populations occasionally experienced harsh behaviours (73.04 per cent) from their fellow adult employees. But significant proportion (22.96 per cent) of them had frequently met harsh behaviours from the fellow adult employees while very few of them (4.00 per cent) had not experienced harsh behaviours from the fellow adult employees. In the Control Group this trend was almost identical with 72.95 per cent of these wage earning children had occasionally experienced harsh behaviours from their fellow adult employees and another 23.04 per cent had frequently met harsh behaviours from their fellow adult employees. In the Programme Group, on the other hand, all the wage earning children occasionally experienced harsh treatments from their fellow adult employees.

The author also studied the distribution of the wage earning child labourer according to the employer's behaviour in the workplaces (Table 3.10.44). This distribution revealed that most (73.04 per cent) of the child labourers in All Populations had occasionally faced harsh behaviours from their employers and significant proportion of them (22.96 per cent) had frequently met harsh behaviours from their employers. Only 4.00 per cent of these wage earning children did not subjected to harsh behaviours from their employers. In the Control Group this trend was almost similar where 72.95 per cent of the wage earning children had occasionally met harsh behaviours and another 23.04 per cent had frequently met harsh behaviours from their employers while only 4.01 per cent had not faced harsh behaviours from their parents. In the Programme Group, on the other hand, all the wage earning children had occasionally faced harsh behaviours from their employers.

Distribution of the *child labourers according to the mode of receiving wage or income* (Table 3.10.45) showed that most of the child labourers in All Populations (54.02 per cent) received weekly wages or incomes whereas a very high proportion of them (26.93 per cent) received daily wages or incomes and few

(7.12 per cent) received monthly wages or incomes. Many child labourers (11.92 per cent to be precise) were engaged in the family businesses or enterprises and therefore did not have any tangible income or wage. In the Control Group one could find an almost identical trend of the mode of receiving wage or income where 54.15 per cent child labourers received weekly wages/incomes, 27.23 per cent daily wages/incomes and 7.20 per cent monthly wages/incomes. In the Programme Group, on the other hand, child labourers were either engaged in the family enterprises or businesses (57.14 per cent) thus did not receive any wage/income or receive weekly wages/incomes (42.86 per cent).

The popular notion that the child labourers generally do not have any family, which may in fact be true for some other Third World cities, proved to be completely wrong at least for this study in Kolkata. Thus the distribution of the *child labourers according to the presence or absence of family* (Table 3.10.46) showed that all the child labourers in All Populations had their own families and this distribution was valid for both the Control Group and the Programme Group.

The author also found that the distribution of the *child labourers according to the contribution of income towards their households* (Table 3.10.47) reflected that most of the child labourers in All Populations were either contributing (65.48 per cent) more than fifty per cent of their earnings or between ten to fifty per cent of their earnings (18.42 per cent). Some of them (11.30 per cent) were contributing less than ten per cent of their earnings to their households and even fewer (4.80 per cent) were contributing nothing to their households. In the Control Group this trend was almost similar with 65.26 per cent of the child labourers reportedly were contributing more than fifty per cent of the earning, 18.47 per cent between ten to fifty per cent of the earning, 11.42 per cent less than ten per cent of the earning and 4.85 per cent were contributing nothing to their households. In the Programme Group in most cases (85.71 per cent) the entire earnings of the child labourers were reportedly going to the family and in 14.29 per cent of the cases ten to fifty per cent of the earnings were going to the family.

The distribution of the *child labourers according to the level of dependence of the household on his/her income* (Table 3.10.48) again showed that in most cases (71.21 per cent) in All Populations dependence was substantial. In many other cases (23.53 per cent) the dependence was nominal and in few cases (4.80 per cent) there was no dependence of the households on the income of the child labourers. On the other hand, in many cases (0.46 per cent) the families were entirely dependent on their working children's incomes. In the Control Group similar trend of dependence was found where 71.05 per cent of the child labourers' families were substantially dependent on their incomes, 23.32 per cent nominally dependent, 4.85 per cent not dependent and 0.47 per cent were completely dependent on their incomes. In the Programme Group these families were either substantially dependent (57.14 per cent) or nominally dependent (42.86 per cent) on their working children's incomes.

Distribution of the *child labour population according to the level of his/her own spending from his/her earning* (Table 3.10.49) also revealed that the majority (60.53 per cent) of the child labourers in All Populations were spending less than ten per cent of their earnings for their own purposes while 15.01 per cent were spending between ten to fifty per cent of their earnings and 19.66 per cent spending more than fifty per cent of their earnings. Some of them (4.80 per cent) were also spending the entire amount of their earnings to meet their own needs. Among the child labourers in the Control Group similar trend of spending was found with 60.88 per cent were spending less than ten per cent of their earnings on themselves, 14.40 per cent were spending between ten per cent to fifty per cent of their earnings and 19.87 per cent were spending more than fifty per cent of their earnings to meet their own needs while 4.85 per cent were spending their entire earnings on themselves. In the Programme Group, however, the child labourers were spending between ten per cent to fifty per cent (71.43 per cent) of their income or less than ten per cent (28.57 per cent) of their earnings to meet their needs.

The author also studied the distribution of these *child labourers according to the frequency of leaving job* (Table 3.10.50) which indicated that most of the child labourers in All Populations had never left (44.89 per cent) or left just once (34.52 per cent) the job. Many of them, however, had left their jobs two to five times (14.09 per cent) or even more than five times (6.50 per cent). In the Control Group 44.76 per cent of the child labourers had never left their job and 34.59 per cent left just once while 14.08 per cent left two to five times and 42 per cent had left their jobs for more than five times. In the Programme Group, on the contrary, most of the child labourers either had never left their jobs (57.14 per cent) or just left just once (28.57 per cent).

The author also studied the distribution of *child labourers according to the reason for leaving job* (Table 3.10.51) and found that in most cases the child labourers in All Populations who were working in intolerable working conditions (14.86 per cent) or with very low pay (13.78 per cent) or had accident-prone jobs (11.42 per cent) forced to leave their jobs more frequently. Other reasons for leaving jobs included getting fired or terminated (8.20 per cent), or to learn a skilled and more lucrative job (3.10 per cent), or due to too much distance to the workplace (2.63 per cent) or due to some other reasons like abuse, boredom of the job, etc. (1.25 per cent). In the Control Group similar trend was found where 15.02 per cent had left the job due to intolerable working conditions, 13.46 per cent for very low pay, 11.42 per cent for accident proneness of the job, 8.29 per cent got fired or terminated, 3.13 per cent left the job to learn a skilled and more lucrative job, 2.66 per cent due to too much distance to the workplace and 1.25 per cent for some other reasons. In the Programme Group, on the other hand, all the child labourers who had left their jobs attributed the reason to very low pay (42.86 per cent).

One can see from these quantitative accounts that the child labour is not an isolated phenomenon. On the contrary, it is inextricably bound with various other socio-economic factors like the level of marginality of the families, literacy standard of the parents as well as the children, economic condition of the families and various other factors associated with the marginalised families and beyond the control of those families.

The condition of child labourers was also investigated in detail with various important quantitative parameters among the working children like literacy standard, occupational details like the nature of work, working condition, earning and spending level, the degree of dependence of the households on the income of its working children, facilities available in the workplaces, etc. The author found that in the Programme Group, which was benefited from the programme of security of tenure for two decades before the commencement of this study, had almost solved the problem of child labour as the proportion of child labourer in this group was negligible. In the Control Group, where there were no security of tenure and the people were living under constant threat of eviction, the situation of child labour had worsened. Child labourers from these two groups had also differed on the type of work they were engaged with as the child labourers from the Programme Group were more involved in the domestic businesses with flexible working hours and much better working condition while most of the child labourers from the Control Group were wage earners and working under much harsher working condition with longer working hours.

While the quantitative accounts showed the contrasting condition of child labour among two groups of people the author would now discuss the findings of the qualitative accounts of child labour situation in all the settlements in the next section and see how it corroborated the findings from the quantitative accounts.

SECTION VIII—THICK DESCRIPTION OF THE KEY BEHAVIOURS

It has long been argued in our discipline that it is possible for an anthropologist to describe and analyse another culture without having to empathise with people. Anthropologists seek to understand the "webs of significance" which people weave within the cultural context, and these webs of significance can be communicated to others mainly by thickly describing the situation and its context. In the earlier sections of this chapter the author, along with the analysis of frequency distributions, has given excerpts of various case studies which were also part of the thick descriptions that helped to provide depth in many observations and situations. The author, in his quest for the further insights through qualitative and/or intensive aspects of the present study, also resorted to the thick descriptions of some of the key behaviours observed during this fieldwork. It became imperative for this work as detailed quantitative accounts as well as case studies of the people under study might not reflect some of the important aspects of these marginalised people. The author, in doing thick descriptions of the case studies, has already given some directly quoted interjections by the informants. He has also made some direct reproductions of his fieldnotes, as he tried to understand some of the key behaviours of the studied populations through thick descriptions to reflect the webs of significance in a translucent way. Thus, the author tried to give a comparative picture of some of the key behaviours of the Population-I and II (i.e. the Control Group) as well as the Population-III (i.e. the Programme Group).

(A) Contrasting Social Position of the Children in Two Groups

It was observed during this fieldwork in the Control Group that the children were often been physically beaten by both the parents even on trivial issues. It was also observed that the children over the breast-feeding age used to be left alone by their mothers while the latter worked and gossiped. Children of every age played in unhygienic (dirty) conditions and the parents were indifferent to the unhygienic conditions in which their children played. Male children received preferential treatment compared to the female children by both the parents. Observations were made during this fieldwork regarding the preferential treatment to male children by the parents and the author found in the Control Group like the male children got with better or larger share of the food, male children did not have to do the household works, the demands of the male children were taken care of more than the female children and the parents were more willing to forgive the pranks of the male children. It was also observed that the earning children sometimes received kinder treatments from their parents than the non-earning children. Thus the earning children in some cases were served with better or larger part of the food, they could demand money for recreational activities, they received more protection from both the parents for their many misdeeds, and they were allowed more reprieves from the household works. It was also observed during this fieldwork that the school going children in the Control Group used to read most of their lessons in daylight. Reading after the dusk was almost impossible in these two settlements as there were no electricity present in both the settlements and the cost of burning lamp was too high for these people. Children were almost always encouraged to respond to all types of nature's call on the open space mostly on the side of the metal road. Children often eat food in unhygienic (dirty) conditions. Immunising their own children was not on the most priority list among the parents in both the settlements as they could not understand the importance of immunisation. But in the cases where children received doses of immunisation, mothers carried their children to the nearby immunising centre.

In the Programme Group it was observed that the school-going children (both boys and girls) read their lessons both during the daytime and after dusk. This was possible due to the presence of electricity in most of the households in this settlement. Another factor which rendered this fact possible was the high importance of education of children attached by their parents in the Programme Group. Physical beating of the children by their parents was also common in the Programme Group but not always on trivial issues. Small children strolling and playing in dirty conditions could also be seen in this population but this picture was much rarer than observed the Control Group. Children both of the breast-feeding age and over the breast-feeding age were properly taken care of by their mothers till they reached an age around 10 years, to play separately with their peers. But mostly the children under five years of age always were stuck with their mothers. In the Programme Group also, the male children got preferential treatments compared to the female children by both the parents. For example, male children were served with better and/or larger part of the food, they did not have to do most of the household works, their demands were more easily taken care of than the female children, and boys were more easily forgiven for their mischievous activities. Even the mischief of boys was somewhat overlooked as it became a kind of taken for granted reality for these people that the boys would do such mischievous works but girls were not allowed to anything resembling mischievous activities. In the Programme Group children defecating on the open space was also a somewhat common scene but many families had their own toilets leading to the discontinuation of this practice. Children taking food in unhygienic conditions was not so common picture here as they were taught from the very beginning that this practice would not be good for the health and the children who were doing such things usually get punishments. Immunising children was an almost universal feature here and the mothers were found to be carrying their children to the immunising centre.

(B) Child Labourers' Own Perceptions on the Reason of their Working

The author made some observations on the child labourers' own perceptions about the reason for their working. Most child labourers thought that the family's inability to continue study was the main reason of their working. Other most cited reasons were their family's need of the contribution, helping their family businesses and the need of money for their own survival. Few child labourers also cited reasons like boredom towards study, learning a skilled and lucrative job and some other reasons like prevalent tradition of the family to work early or blaming destiny, etc. It must also be mentioned here that many working children could not respond properly to the question of their main reason of working.

> I met Kabirul in Population-II, an eleven-year old boy, who used to work in a nearby garage as an apprentice. His father was a contractual worker in a nearby factory and his mother worked as a scrap-sorter in a nearby place. Kabirul had a younger brother and a sister also. His sister (who is elder than Kabirul) also used to work in a house (as domestic help) and was living there. I found that Kabirul had been admitted to a school (non-formal school run by a local NGO) for few months and

> learnt reading and writing skills. Later, according to Kabirul, his father and mother began to think that Kabirul must learn motor-repairing, a skill which had demands in the local market and bring some money to their family. Thus Kabirul stopped going to that school. Kabirul's father established a contact with a nearby motor garage where Kabirul was working now for nearly a year. At about this time, Kabirul's younger brother was born. During the time of my fieldwork Kabirul's father got Rs. 200 each month for Kabirul's work. The garage owner provided Kabirul a morning Tiffin (bread and tea) and Kabirul had to take day's lunch in his own home for which he was allowed to have a break of an hour. Kabirul was learning motor-repairing works. He was hoping to learn the work quickly and one day he was aspiring to become a good and independent motor mechanic.

The above observations were mostly limited in the Control Group. In the Programme Group the problem of child labour was very negligible and where the above responses in this regard went either in favour of family's need of contribution or need to help the family business.

> I spoke to Basanti Manna, a 12 years old girl from Population-III. She was reading in Class IV in a nearby Girls' school during the time of this fieldwork. Her family was associated with a business of incense-sticks. They prepared those incense-sticks in their own house and her father sold those incense-sticks to a middle-man as well as to some local shops. Basanti's mother, father, elder sister and elder brother all used to make incense sticks. They needed more helping hands and thus Basanti learnt how to make those sticks. Basanti joined other family members in making the incense-sticks in the morning and in the evening...i.e. before and after the school hours.... Basanti said that her mother was very particular about her study and did not let her work during the study times. Basanti wanted to continue her study and I also spoke to her mother who also seemed

> to be interested to continue Basanti's study as long as possible.

(C) Parents' Perceptions of the Reason for Working of Their Children

The author observed that the parents of the child labourers responded differently when asked on why their children were working. Most of these parents responded in favour of family's need of a contribution from the child. Other most cited reasons in this regard were the inability of the family to continue the study of their children study, engaging their children apprenticeship to a skilled and lucrative job which had demands in the local market and child's inattentiveness to study. Some other parents of these working children responded that family had not interfered in the child's own decision of working or cited some other reasons like spontaneous decision of working from the family, family tradition of working early from the childhood, etc. Many parents, however, also could not respond properly in this regard.

> I met Nusrat Begum in Population-I who had two sons and a daughter. Her 12 years old elder son worked in a local restaurant as a (helper) boy. Her younger son, who was 10 years old, worked as a scrap-sorter. I asked her why she had let her children work so early. She replied that her husband worked as a porter in a nearby market and earned very little which was insufficient for the family's survival. She was also engaged in some ill-paid low skill jobs like domestic helps, helper in construction works, etc. But together they did not earn enough to meet the expenditures of their household and their family was suffering terribly for this ordeal. Hence they had no other option but to engage their children in work. The small sum of money which the children brought was a great help for their family. They could spend that money in their food, cloth, and for Nusrat's treatment as she had a chronic chest pain (possibly a heart problem) and had to spend many rupees frequently for treatment. When I asked her on the education of her

> children I found that she was of the opinion that the education was of little use in their life. She said that she had seen many educated people who did not have any job. This had led her to realise that educating her children would not serve their purpose which was day-to-day survival. Despite her opinion against education she admitted her elder child was admitted to a nearby (non-formal) school for few months and the boy learned how to sign his name. But I found that both Nusrat and her husband were of firm opinion that their children needed to work to support the family.

(D) Employers' Responses on Employing Children in Their Establishments

The author found that the employers' responses on the reasons for putting children to work in their establishments were equally variegated. During this fieldwork, most of these employers said unequivocally that they employed the children to help their families and explained that they could not turn down the requests of the parents. According to some of the employers working children were obedient, had skills that were compatible with certain jobs and could be hired at lower wages. The author also found that some employers did not respond properly in this regard.

> I met Saif Ahmed, a 55 years old motor repairing garage (workshop) owner in the Rajabazar in the central part of Kolkata, where two children from Population-II were employed. According to Saif, he had ten adult employees and two children in his garage. These two children were working as helpers in different garage works. They were learning the repairing job now. Saif added that a number of his child employees had obtained jobs in other garages or become independent motor mechanics after learning how to repair motor cars. Saif said that he did have few other children who after learning the repairing works left his garage. Those children later became independent motor mechanic or were employed in other garages. So it was proved to be

> a rather bad investment for him. Saif exclaimed that the fathers of these children came to him and requested him to keep their children in his garage as helpers so that they could learn the skill of motor repairing. He explained that he employed those children to help their families and it proved to be a futile investment for him as he had to provide the children with food in the morning and the daytime. He also gave some money to their parents. On asking further he said that he did not know about any child labour prevention law. He even promised me that the day he would learn about any such law, he would terminate these children.

(E) Leisure Time Activities of the Child Labourers

During the fieldwork, the author also made few observations on the leisure time activities of the child labourers. Child labourers spent their leisure time by chatting or listening to radios. Some child labourers were fond of watching cinema. Other leisure time activities of the child labourers included watching television placed in the neighbours' house or in some roadside shops and occasionally smoking cigarettes.

> I met Manzoor Alam, a twelve years old boy living in Population-II who was a scrap-picker. He said to me that he started working before dawn as starting work afterwards was futile because other scrap-pickers picked everything worth collecting. Generally he used to come back to his settlement at the early afternoon after collecting the scraps. But collecting scrap was only part of the job. He then used to go to the nearby scrap-buyer to sell those scraps before returning home. Only after selling the daily collection of scraps he could eat and rest. He used to spend the evenings leisurely. I also found during more than one evening that he was listening to Hindi songs in radio and was chatting with one of his friends. He said that he was very much fond of watching Hindi movies in television or theatre. According to Manzoor, he generally watched at least one movie in a week in a nearby theatre. Sometimes, as

> he said, he watched cricket matches and movies in television in a nearby shop.

(F) Child Labourers' Own Perceptions on Their Reality

The child labourers' own perception about their own reality was an extremely important issue in this work. The author spent a lot of time with child labourers in an effort to gauge their own perceptions. The author found that in most of the cases child labourers described their life as very harsh and full of financial and physical constraints. But on further observations it was also found that most of these child labourers were of opinion that they must accept the life in its present form as they were left with no other alternative, while a minority said that they could not accept their reality.

> I met Bhuban in Population-II several times during various hours of the day and in the evenings. Bhuban was a 12 years old scrap-picker. His working day began before the dawn and which continued till the late afternoon. He used to get rest only after he had sold the day's collections to the scrap-dealer. He said that he had body aches each day after his return from the collection. Cuts on his hands and feet were very common as he had to go to the places where the broken glasses and sharp objects remained scattered. Bhuban narrated a recent incident when he had a deep cut on his right feet and was bleeding profusely. But he could not get any treatment from the local people. He had to wrap his wound himself with his (dirty) cloth. He wrapped the wound and came back to his home where he got some dressings from a local 'doctor' (paramedics). Bhuban showed me that wound which was still deep and not entirely healed. I found that Bhuban was working in dirty conditions with his unhealed wounds. He said that the people from other neighbourhoods consider scrap-pickers like him as potential thieves or lifters. Dog bites and chasing were common to his life. But he was compelled to do (this) work as his father was not earning much from his work as a porter.

> Bhuban's mother had worked as a scrap-sorter and received very low wage. Bhuban also had two more brothers to feed. Bhuban contributed most of his earned money to his father who managed the regular expenses of their household. During my fieldwork period I found that Bhuban's father started looking for a better job for him as he was in contact with a local motor repairing garage (workshop). His father hoped that in a month or two, Bhuban would join the garage as an apprentice to motor repairing work.

Many of these child labourers considered their working life as a better one than their early life since they were starving less. The work also brought provisions of some kind of savings and it brought little more varieties in life. The author found that some of these child labourers could not respond properly in this respect.

> I met Arif, a 13 years old scrap-picker from Population-I, for the first time during the initial stages of my fieldwork in Population-I. After the initial meet, Arif became a good friend of mine and worked as a key informant in my fieldwork. Most of the times, I went to the field during the afternoons and Arif used to introduce me with other people in the settlement. With the passage of time during my fieldwork, I found that Arif could be a key informant for me. One day I was chatting with Arif and asked him about his own life. He said that his father was suffering from respiratory diseases and was ill for most of the time during the year. Arif's father did not have any steady income throughout the year. His mother was working as a domestic help in some nearby houses. Arif had one more brother who also was working as a scrap-picker with him. According to Arif, life for all the members of his household was better now though he considered his work as a backbreaking one. Earlier, the family had to starve frequently when his father was not able to work and their mother's income got exhausted by the second week of the month. Now that both the brothers were

working and bringing some money, it brought some relief to the family.

(G) Child Labourers' Own Perceptions on Their Future

The author also tried to comprehend the child labourers' own perceptions on their future. Many child labourers were interviewed in different times during this fieldwork and their lives were observed for long durations. Most of the child labourers considered that some change could happen in their life by which they meant that they expected a better earning to support their families. Others hoped that they might find a job where the wages were better or might find a better future in other cities like Delhi or Mumbai. But a substantial proportion of them considered that no perceptible change could happen in their life which might result amelioration in their situation.

> I met Kaimur, a 13 years old child labourer in Population-I, several times during my fieldwork. At that time he was working in a motor repairing garage (workshop). I went to the garage where he was working and also interviewed his employer. Kaimur said that when he started this work he did not know anything and had to endure frequent beatings from the owner and the fellow adult employee. Slowly he became acquainted with the repairing tools as well as different intricacies of motor car and motorcycle repairing. According to Kaimur, he could now do various types of repairing jobs by himself. Initially his father received Rs. 500 per month for Kaimur's work. During this fieldwork he was getting Rs. 1200 per month from the owner. Kaimur sometimes received the part of the tips from the owners of the car. Kaimur said that he had also received extra rewards from the owner during the festival times like Bakri-Id. I found that he could drive cars as well as motorbikes. I also found that both his parents and one of his brothers were also working. Kaimur hoped to become a full-fledged motor mechanic soon. Kaimur said that the only work he needed to know was the how to repair the engine, which (according

to Kaimur) was very difficult to learn. He hoped to open his own roadside repairing shop one day and repairing motorcycles and motor cars. He had an aspiration to earn more money and create a better life for himself as well as for his family.

Thus the above comparative picture of some of the key behaviours in the Control Group and the Programme Group revealed that the Programme Group was in far better position as far as the marginalisation of population and the condition of child labourers were concerned. It also revealed various unexplored aspects on the worldviews of the child labourers, their parents and the employers of child labourers. In the next section the author made some statistical observations on the level of urban marginality in all the three populations where the author conducted some statistical analyses on a few randomly selected households in each population group to understand the differences in the condition of marginality among the Control Group and the Programme Group.

SECTION IX—STATISTICAL ANALYSES ON THE MARGINALISATION OF POPULATION AND CHILD LABOUR

The author conducted statistical analyses on these populations to see whether we can draw any statistical correlation between the marginalisation of population and child labour. This study also investigated whether the hypothesis of equality as far as collective consumption and other social chances concerned was holding true among the two groups. In this effort, the author randomly selected 10 families each from the Population I and Population II (i.e. the Control Group) and 20 families from the Population-III (i.e. the Programme Group). Following observations were made on these families and the author put weighted scores according to findings in those families.

Level of Urban Marginalisation

The level of urban marginalisation was gauged here on the basis of legitimacy of the houses occupied as well as the housing conditions and other facilities like latrine and drinking water.

Table 3.9.1: The Aspects to be Observed on Urban Marginalisation

LEGITIMACY OF THE HOUSE OCCUPIED	SCORE
Living on an illegally occupied land	1
Living on a legally occupied land	2
HOUSING CONDITION	
Katcha house with water permeable roof	1
Katcha house with water impermeable roof	2
Semi pucca with water permeable roof	3
Semi pucca with water impermeable roof	4
Pucca with water permeable roof	5
Pucca with water impermeable roof	6
NATURE OF HOUSING	
Living on a illegally occupied land with below 30 sq. meters plinth area	1
Living on a illegally occupied land with 30 sq. meters or above plinth area	2
Living on a legally occupied land with below 30 sq. meters plinth area	3
Living on a legally occupied land with 30 sq. meters or above plinth area	4
LATRINE FACILITY	
No latrine	1
Service latrine	2
Makeshift latrine	3
Community latrine with septic tank	4
Family latrine with septic tank	5
Family latrine with flush system	6
DRINKING WATER SOURCES	
Open reservoir, pond or canal	1
Community tube-wells or handpumps	2
Family tube-wells or handpumps	3
Community tap	4
Family tap	5

Legitimacy of the House Occupied

All the 20 households of the Control Group were occupying the land or the shelter for which they or their landlords did not have any legitimate right. On the other hand, all the 20 households of the Programme Group were legitimately occupying the houses or the portion of the houses they were occupying i.e. though the ownership of land of their housing structures were not there for the occupier or their landlords but their housing structures were owned by the occupier or their landlords under the Calcutta *Thika* and Other Tenancies and Lands (Acquisition and Regulation) Act (1981). This difference in legitimacy of the occupation clearly indicates that the population of the first set (i.e. the Control Group) was financially in a greater hardship and was compelled to occupying in less secured and less expensive accommodation. This group, where the inhabitants could not afford to be concerned about the legitimacy of their houses occupied, was clearly more marginalized financially as well as in terms of the urban space in the city of Kolkata and eventually became evicted from the place they were occupying. But the situation in the Programme Group of population was quite different as the inhabitants in that settlements were found to have the required legitimacy of their houses occupied and could not get evicted until the repealing or the amendment of the concerned act annulling their *Thika* tenancy rights.

Housing Condition and Some Collective Consumption Facilities

As mentioned earlier, housing condition and some collective consumption facilities like nature of housing, latrine facility and drinking water sources (for the details of these parameters and the scores thereof see table 5.9.3) which were necessary for day-to-day living were identified and scores assigned to those according to their level of convenience and quality. The results for each of the 20 sampled households from the Control Group and the other 20 households from the Programme Group are shown in the Tables 3.9.1 and 3.9.2.

Table 3.9.2: Housing Condition and Some Collective Consumption Facilities in the Control Group

Family No.	Housing Condition	Nature of Housing	Latrine Facility	Drinking Water Source
POPULATION-I				
140	1	1	1	4
114	1	2	1	4
59	1	2	1	4
11	1	2	3	4
17	2	2	3	4
171	1	1	4	2
32	2	2	3	4
136	2	2	1	2
48	1	2	1	4
31	1	2	1	2
POPULATION-II				
131	1	2	3	4
266	2	1	3	4
258	1	1	3	4
358	1	1	3	2
231	1	2	1	4
13	2	2	3	4
202	3	2	3	4
133	1	2	3	4
344	1	1	3	4

Now the question is whether, so far as housing condition and these collective consumption facilities are concerned, the population groups got any distinctive features. To test this some statistical tools have been performed.

The author tested the equality of the means for the two sets of population (i.e. the Control Group and the Programme Group) as follows:

Housing Condition and Some Collective Consumption Facility	Population-I & II (Control Group)		Population-III (Programme Group)	
	Mean	Standard Deviation	Mean	Standard Deviation
1. Condition of Housing	1.37	0.56	4.05	0.74
2. Nature of Housing	1.68	0.47	1.65	0.48
3. Latrine Facility	2.32	1.03	4.55	0.59
4. Drinking Water Source	3.58	0.82	4.15	0.65

A. Housing condition

z = 12.62 Highly significant (| z |? 1.96)

B. Nature of housing

z = 0.197 Significant at 5% level (| z |? 2.58 at 1%)

C. Latrine facility
z = 8.24 Highly significant (| z |? 2.58 at 1%)

D. Drinking water
z = 2.40 Significant at 5% level (| z |? 1.96)

Table 3.9.3: Housing Condition and Some Collective Consumption Facilities in the Programme Group

Family No.	Housing Condition	Nature of Housing	Latrine Facility	Drinking Water Source
POPULATION-III				
163	4	1	4	4
168	4	2	4	4
70	4	1	4	4
40	3	1	5	4
127	4	2	4	5
205	4	2	5	4
17	3	2	5	4
42	6	2	5	4
111	4	1	5	4
122	4	2	5	4
207	4	2	5	4
148	4	2	4	4
158	4	2	4	4
31	4	1	4	5
182	4	2	4	3
100	3	1	5	4
36	4	2	5	4
203	4	2	6	4
4	4	1	4	4
187	6	2	4	4

Following conclusions can be drawn from the above tests.

(a) Condition of housing for the Programme Group was significantly better than that of the other population group (i.e. the Control Group).

(b) A difference between the available housing accommodations for two groups of population was quite discernable and the Programme Group was enjoying the better of it.

(c) Similarly, the available latrine facility of the Programme Group was of significantly improved type than that was in use by the other group i.e. the Control Group.

(d) Though the access to drinking water facility should be the same for all groups of population in an area, the hypothesis of equality of mean score on this count was observed to be significant at 5 per cent level, indicating the rejection of null hypothesis at 5 per cent level of significance i.e. the data indicate that the Programme Group got better access to drinking water than the Control Group of populations when they used to live in the studied places.

Participation of Children in Economic Activity

The author also studied that on that trend of participation of the children in economic activity among in both the population groups. Among these studied population groups, at least the first two (i.e. the Population-I and II or the Control Group) belonged mostly to the weaker section. Non-participation in schooling and participation of adolescent children in economic activity (child labour) was prevalent among the poorer section the Control Group. The inferences which can be drawn from the following tests focus on these aspects.

The information tabulated here relating to 10 households of each of the Control Group of populations, and 20 households of the Programme Group have been summarized in the following two 2 × 2 contingency tables.

Summary Table 1

Population Group	Whether the Children of the Households Participating in Economic Activity		Total
	Yes	No	
Population-I and II	13	7	20
Population-III	2	18	20
Total	15	25	40

Summary Table 2

Population Group	Whether the Children of the Households Going to School		Total
	Yes	No	
Population-I and II	5	15	20
Population-III	18	2	20
Total	23	17	40

Test 1: Let it be assumed that there was no association between the studied population groups and the extent of participation of children in economic activity that is, the null hypothesis.

From the Summary Table - 1, the value of Chi-Square

$X^2 = 14.7$

The value of X^2 with one degree of freedom at 1 per cent probability is

$X^2.01, 1 = 6.6$

The observed value of $X^2 = 14.7$ is quite large at 1 per cent level of significance. Hence there is good reason to infer that there was much higher propensity of children of the Control Group to enter into the labour market and the tendency was comparatively much low among children of the Programme Group.

Test 2: As in Test 1, the null hypothesis in this case is the non-existence of any association between the extents of participation of children in schools in three population groups.

From the Summary Table - 2, the value of

$X^2 = 10.7$ and as already observed the value of X^2 with one degree of freedom at 1 per cent probability is

$X^2.01, 1 = 6.6$

The observed value of 10.7 being much higher than that at 1 per cent level of significance the null hypothesis of no association has to be rejected. It may, therefore, be inferred that the children of the Programme Group were keener to go to school than their Control Group counterpart.

NOTES

1. According to UNICEF [2002], crude birth rate is the annual number of births per 1000 population. The lack of proper birth registration system in India does not allow calculating the crude birth rate properly which also holds true for this study.
2. Total Fertility Rate is defined as the numbers of children a woman have if hypothetically she lived through her reproductive years i.e. 15-49 years, experiencing the age specific fertility rates prevailing in the population during a given period, RGI (1999a).

3. Total Fertility Rate (calculated according to the number of children) in India during 1995-97 was 3.4 (2.7 in West Bengal) compared to 1990-92 when it was 3.7 (3.2 in West Bengal). For urban India the rate was 2.5 in 1995-97 (1.8 in West Bengal) and 2.7 in 1990-92 (2.0 in West Bengal) (RGI, 1999a).
4. Infant Mortality Rate is defined as the number of death by age 1 per 1000 live births. For urban India this rate was as high as 51 per thousand whereas for urban West Bengal the rate was little lower i.e. 41 per thousand, according to 1991 census data (RGI 1997).
5. As per 1991 census, in India Child-Woman Ratio (0-4) in urban areas is 428 children per 1000 women aged 15-49 years whereas in urban West Bengal the figure stands lower i.e. 317 children per 1000 women aged 15-49 years (RGI 1991).
6. CWR (0-4) in Population-I was particularly high i.e. 1321 children per 1000 women aged 15-49 years. The reason behind this high CWR (0-4) in Population-I may be due to the fact that this population was in a sort of flux in view of an ensuing eviction.
7. According to 1991 census CWR (5-9) in urban India is 549 children per 1000 women aged 15-49 years and in urban West Bengal CWR (5-9) is 456 children per 1000 women aged 15-49 years (RGI, 1991).
8. CWR (5-9) in Population-I was particularly high (1560 children per 1000 women aged 15-49 years) due to the same possibility as mentioned in the preceding footnote.
9. Author preferred the term 'non-literate' than the frequently used one in this regard i.e. the 'illiterate'.
10. Literacy Rate is defined as the proportion of literates to the population in the age group 7+ (RGI, 2001).
11. According to 2001 census, in India 65.20 per cent and in West Bengal 69.22 per cent are literates. In the urban settings the national rate of literacy is 80.06 per cent whereas the rate of literacy in urban areas in West Bengal is 81.63. Female literacy rate in India is even lower i.e. 54.03 per cent in West Bengal this rate is somewhat higher i.e. 60.22 per cent. In the urban areas the female literacy rate in India is 72.99 per cent and in West Bengal 76.14 per cent (RGI, 2001).

12. According to the Census of India (2001), the literacy rate is defined as the proportion of literates to total population in the age group 7 years and above.
13. The literacy rate was merely 18.3 per cent (for the age group 5 years and above) in 1951, 43.6 per cent in 1981 (for the age group 5 years and above) and is 65.2 per cent as per the Census 2001. There are, however, large inter-State variations in literacy rates in the country. At one end, proportion of literates was the highest in Kerala, at over 90 per cent, and at the other it was less than 50 per cent in Bihar for the year 2001. The regional variations in literacy rates have declined since 1981, though the disparities become more pronounced if one takes into account rural-urban differences or the differences between male and female literacy rates. In the urban areas it is 80.06 per cent compared to 59.21 per cent in the rural areas. On the other hand, according to 2001 census, male literacy in India is 75.64 per cent in comparison to 54.03 per cent literacy among the females.
14. In West Bengal, as per the 2001 census, the overall literacy rate is 69.22 per cent and the urban literacy rate is 81.63 per cent compared to the rural literacy rate of 64.06 per cent.
15. According to 53rd round NSSO calculations the national literacy rate is 62 per cent compared to a higher 72 per cent in the state of West Bengal. In the urban areas the national rate of literacy is 80 per cent whereas in urban West Bengal this rate is 83 per cent (NSSO, 2001).
16. As per the 2001 census male literacy rate in combined areas is 75.64 per cent (77.78 per cent in West Bengal) and the corresponding female literacy rate is 54.03 per cent (60.22 per cent in West Bengal). In urban India this male literacy is 86.42 per cent (86.49 per cent in the urban areas of West Bengal) whereas the female literacy rate in urban India is 72.99 per cent (76.14 per cent in urban West Bengal).
17. According to 53rd round NSSO calculations the national male literacy rate is 73 per cent (81 per cent in West Bengal) and female literacy rate is 50 per cent (63 per cent in West Bengal). In urban areas of India the male literacy rate is 88 per cent (90 per cent in urban West Bengal) and 72 per cent among the females (76 per cent among the females in urban West Bengal).
18. Child literacy rate is percentage of literates in age-group 7-14 years to population in that age group.

19. According to 1991 census data this child literacy rate in India is 64.16 per cent and in West Bengal this rate is 62.56 per cent (RGI, 1999c).
20. Again 1991 census data shows that the male child literacy rate in India is 71.44 per cent (67.21 per cent in West Bengal) and female child literacy rate is 56.57 per cent (44.02 per cent in West Bengal) (RGI, 1999c).
21. The concept of collective consumption has already been discussed earlier.
22. During the time of fieldwork the state of Jharkhand was not created.
23. In India people over the age of 18 years are regarded as eligible for voting in any election.
24. Author, unlike economists, considered every working person (child or adult) in the labour force.
25. According to NSS 55th round study in 1999-2000, 61.8 per cent (55.0 per cent in West Bengal) persons in India is in labour force. In the urban areas the national figure of persons in labour force is 51.1 per cent and in the state 50.5 per cent is in labour force (NSSO, 2001).
26. In India 83.5 per cent (84.6 per cent in West Bengal) of the male persons are in labour force and 38.5 per cent (22.2 per cent in West Bengal) female persons are in labour force. In the urban Indian areas 78.6 per cent males (80.5 per cent in West Bengal) are in labour force and 20.9 per cent females (16.5 per cent in West Bengal) (NSSO, 2001).
27. According to NSSO 55th Round study during 1999-2000, in India the unemployment rate is 2.3 per cent (4.0 per cent in West Bengal) and in urban India this rate is 4.8 per cent (7.6 per cent in urban West Bengal). Gender-wise distribution of the unemployment rate shows that among the Indian males 2.5 per cent is unemployed (3.9 in West Bengal) and 1.8 per cent of the Indian females (4.3 per cent in West Bengal) are unemployed. In urban India 4.5 per cent males (7.2 per cent in West Bengal) are unemployed in comparison to 5.9 of the female-folk (9.7 per cent) are unemployed.
28. According to 1991 census data 5.4 per cent children in India (4.2 per cent in West Bengal) found to working. Of these children 5.7 per cent (5.6 per cent in West Bengal) are boys and 5.1 per cent (5.1 per cent in West Bengal) are girls (RGI, 1998).

29. As per the same census data of 1991 in urban India 2.0 per cent children (1.9 per cent in West Bengal) are found to be working, of them 2.8 per cent are males (2.4 per cent in West Bengal) and 1.2 per cent females (1.3 per cent in West Bengal).
30. Poverty line is officially measured in India as Rupees per capita per month.
31. According to Planning Commission data in urban India the poverty line is Rs. 454.11 per capita per month during 1999-2000 while in urban West Bengal it is Rs. 409.22 per capita per month.
32. Although the frequencies differed appreciably in percentages, in numerical terms the difference of occurrences between the boys and girls among the child labourers was only 1.
33. Drop-out rate is the percentage of students dropping out of class/ classes in a given year. Along with students repeating a class, the drop-out rate gives an indication about the wastage of school education and tends to undermine benefits of increased enrolments.
34. According to the 1998-99 annual report of Department of Education (provisional data) drop-out rate in the class I-V in India is 39.58 per cent (49.92 per cent in West Bengal) of them 38.23 per cent are boys (46.17 per cent in West Bengal) and 41.58 per cent are girls (54.15 per cent in West Bengal).
35. In case the child labourer was engaged in the family enterprise where no payment of wage was done, the daily income calculation was done from the estimation of the market price of the amount of production the child could give to the family enterprise and this estimation was done with the help of the head of that enterprise.

SECTION X—TABLES

Table 3.10.1: Distribution of the Populations According to Age and Sex (Percentages)

Age	Population-I			Population-II			Population-I & II			Population-III			All Populations		
Group	M	F	T	M	F	T	M	F	T	M	F	T	M	F	T
0 - 4	9.76	9.46	19.22	12.13	6.44	18.57	11.34	7.47	18.81	3.86	2.62	6.48	9.50	6.28	15.78
5 - 9	11.76	10.96	22.72	7.86	7.73	15.59	9.18	8.82	18.00	4.27	4.27	8.54	7.97	7.70	15.67
10 - 14	14.30	12.16	26.46	5.56	5.35	10.91	8.50	7.65	16.15	6.48	4.00	10.48	8.01	6.75	14.76
15 - 19	3.47	3.74	7.21	2.85	3.05	5.90	3.06	3.28	6.34	4.55	4.27	8.82	3.43	3.53	6.96
20 - 24	3.34	3.34	6.68	1.28	4.48	5.76	1.98	4.36	6.34	4.69	7.31	12.00	2.65	5.09	7.74
25 - 29	2.94	3.61	6.55	3.05	4.68	7.73	3.01	4.32	7.33	6.07	6.07	12.14	3.77	4.75	8.52
30 - 34	2.00	1.74	3.74	2.71	4.47	7.18	2.47	3.55	6.02	3.86	4.69	8.55	2.82	3.83	6.65
35 - 39	1.74	1.47	3.21	4.48	5.97	10.45	3.69	4.01	7.70	5.10	3.45	8.55	4.04	3.87	7.91
40 - 44	1.20	0.40	1.60	3.59	3.25	6.84	2.80	2.29	5.09	4.27	2.62	6.89	3.16	2.37	5.53
45 - 49	0.93	0.27	1.20	2.78	0.95	3.73	2.17	0.72	2.89	1.79	2.48	4.27	2.07	1.15	3.22
50 - 54	0.40	0.13	0.53	2.44	0.61	3.05	1.75	0.45	2.20	2.62	1.79	4.41	1.97	0.78	2.75
55 - 59	0.27	0.13	0.40	1.36	0.41	1.77	0.98	0.31	1.29	1.51	1.24	2.75	2.49	1.55	4.04
60+	0.40	0.00	0.40	1.42	1.52	2.94	1.08	0.76	1.84	3.09	2.90	5.99	4.17	3.66	7.83
ALL	52.54	47.46	100.00	51.68	48.32	100.00	52.01	47.99	100.00	52.27	47.73	100.00	52.07	47.93	100.00
No. of Persons	748 (100.00)			1475 (100.00)			2223 (100.00)			725 (100.00)			2948 (100.00)		

Table 3.10.2: Distribution of the Populations According to Child-Woman Ratio (0-4 Years)

Population	No. of Children in the Age Group 0-4 Years (A)	No. of Women in the Age Group 15-49 Years (B)	Child-Woman Ratio (A/B × 1000)
Population-I	144	109	1321
Population-II	274	392	699
Population-I & II	418	501	834
Population-III	47	224	210
All Populations	465	725	641

Table 3.10.3: Distribution of the Populations According to Child-Woman Ratio (5-9 Years)

Population	No. of Children in the Age Group 5-9 Years (A)	No. of Women in the Age Group 15-49 Years (B)	Child-Woman Ratio (A/B × 1000)
Population-I	170	109	1560
Population-II	230	392	587
Population-I & II	400	501	798
Population-III	47	224	210
All Populations	447	727	615

Table 3.10.4: Distribution of the Populations According to Child-Woman Ratios

Population	Child-Woman Ratio 0-4 Years	Child-Woman Ratio 5-9 Years
Population-I	1321	1560
Population-II	699	587
Population-I & II	834	798
Population-III	210	210
All Populations	641	615

Table 3.10.5: Distribution of the Populations According to the Standard of Education

Educational Standard	Population-I & II			Population-III			All Populations		
	M	F	T	M	F	T	M	F	T
Non-Literate	7.24%	28.61%	35.85%	1.79%	5.65%	7.45%	5.90%	22.96%	28.86%
Can Sign Only	14.84%	7.69%	22.54%	2.65%	5.24%	10.90%	12.58%	7.09%	19.67%
I-IV	10.84%	3.51%	14.35%	9.10%	9.93%	19.03%	10.41%	5.09%	15.50%
V-VIII	5.31%	0.49%	5.80%	11.72%	13.38%	25.10%	6.89%	3.66%	10.55%
IX-X	1.71%	0.22%	1.93%	5.65%	6.65%	11.86%	2.68%	1.70%	4.38%
Madhyamik/School Final	0.95%	0.00%	0.95%	6.21%	3.44%	9.66%	2.00%	0.85%	2.85%
Higher Secondary	0.00%	0.00%	0.00%	5.65%	0.83%	6.48%	1.39%	0.20%	1.59%
Graduation and/or Above	0.00%	0.00%	0.00%	2.62%	0.41%	2.90%	0.64%	0.10%	0.74%
Possible Literate Total	35.22%	36.62%	71.84%	45.93%	42.62%	88.55%	37.86%	38.09%	75.95%
All Population	52.00%	48.00%	100.00%	52.27%	47.73%	100.00%	52.07%	47.93%	100.00%
No. of Persons	1156	1067	2223	379	346	725	1535	1413	2948

Table 3.10.6: Distribution of the Populations According to the Overall Literacy

Literacy Rate	Population-I & II			Population-III			All Populations		
	M	F	T	M	F	T	M	F	T
Overall Literacy Rate	67.31%	21.15%	44.08%	82.28%	75.40%	78.97%	71.77%	35.78%	54.08%
Literate in Age Group 7+	67.31%	21.15%	44.08%	82.28%	75.40%	78.97%	71.77%	35.78%	54.08%
Non-Literate in Age Group 7+	32.69%	78.85%	55.92%	17.72%	24.60%	21.03%	28.23%	64.22%	46.94%
Total Possible Literate in Age Group 7+	100.00%	100.00%	100.00%	100.00%	100.00%	100.00%	100.00%	100.00%	100.00%
No. of Possible Literate in Age Group 7+	783	837	1597	333	309	642	1116	1146	2239

Table 3.10.7: Distribution of the Populations According to the Child Literacy

Child Literacy	Population-I & II			Population-III			All Populations		
	M	F	T	M	F	T	M	F	T
Child Literacy Rate	74.63%	19.86%	46.75%	98.33%	90.48%	95.10%	78.91%	29.01%	54.27%
Literate Children in Age Group 7-14	74.63%	19.86%	46.75%	98.33%	90.48%	95.10%	78.91%	29.01%	54.27%
Non-Literate Children in Age Group 7-14	25.37%	80.14%	53.25%	1.67%	9.52%	4.90%	21.09%	70.99%	45.73%
Total Possible Literate Children in Age Group 7-14	100.00%	100.00%	100.00%	100.00%	100.00%	100.00%	100.00%	100.00%	100.00%
No. of Possible Child Literate in Age Group 7-14	272	282	554	60	42	102	332	324	656

Table 3.10.8: Distribution of the Populations According to the Place of Birth

Place of Birth	Pop-I	Pop-II	Pop-I & II	Pop-III	All Pops.
Kolkata	23.13%	25.90%	24.97%	73.66%	36.94%
Adjoining districts of Kolkata	7.62%	10.78%	9.72%	12.13%	10.31%
Other districts of West Bengal	2.94%	2.10%	2.38%	1.10%	2.07%
Bihar and Jharkhand	27.14%	26.10%	26.45%	2.07%	20.45%
Uttar Pradesh	0.67%	4.00%	2.88%	0.00%	2.17%
Other states of India	0.93%	6.64%	4.72%	0.14%	3.60%
Bangladesh	37.57%	23.93%	28.52%	10.90%	24.19%
All	100.00%	100.00%	100.00%	100.00%	100.00%
No. of Persons	748	1475	2223	725	2948

Table 3.10.9: Distribution of the Populations According to the Holding of Ration Card

Ration Card Holding	Pop-I	Pop-II	Pop-I & II	Pop-III	All Pops.
Present	0.53%	0.54%	0.54%	72.27%	18.18%
Absent	99.47%	99.46%	99.46%	27.73%	81.82%
All	100.00%	100.00%	100.00%	100.00%	100.00%
No. of Persons	748	1475	2223	725	2948

Table 3.10.10: Distribution of the Populations According to the Voting Status

Voting Status	Pop-I	Pop-II	Pop-I & II	Pop-III	All Pops.
Voter	6.55%	41.83%	29.96%	59.86%	37.31%
Non-Voter	7.62%	8.54%	8.23%	4.41%	7.29%
Total Possible Voter*	22.73%	50.37%	41.07%	64.27%	46.78%
All	100.00%	100.00%	100.00%	100.00%	100.00%
No. of Persons	748	1475	2223	725	2948

*Excludes the population under 18 years of age.

Table 3.10.11: Distribution of the Households According to the Presence of Some Indicators on Collective Consumption

Indicators on Collective Consumption	Households in Pop-I	Households in Pop-II	Households in Pop-I & II	Households Pop-III	Households All Pops.
Accessible primary school within 1 km	100.00%	100.00%	100.00%	100.00%	100.00%
Accessible hospital/ health centre within 1 km	0.00%	0.00%	0.00%	100.00%	28.00%
Accessible playground within 1 km	0.00%	0.00%	0.00%	100.00%	28.00%
Accessible community-centre within 1 km	0.00%	0.00%	0.00%	100.00%	28.00%
Motorable road	100.00%	100.00%	100.00%	100.00%	100.00%
Pucca arterial road within settlement	0.00%	0.00%	0.00%	100.00%	28.00%
Garbage disposal system	0.00%	0.00%	0.00%	100.00%	28.00%
Planned drainage system	0.00%	0.00%	0.00%	100.00%	28.00%
Legally obtained electricity	0.00%	0.00%	0.00%	98.09%	30.13%
Separate ventilation	1.12%	5.26%	3.89%	85.71%	26.80%
Separate family bathroom	0.00%	0.00%	0.00%	29.05%	8.13%
Separate kitchen	1.12%	3.32%	2.59%	64.76%	20.00%
Water impermeable roof	31.29%	34.90%	33.70%	60.48%	41.20%
Water impermeable wall	41.34%	44.05%	43.15%	93.33%	57.20%
Waterlogging of floor during rainy season	66.48%	67.87%	64.41%	3.33%	49.47%
Own household tap as a source of drinking water	0.00%	0.00%	0.00%	10.00%	2.80%
No. of Households	179 (100.00%)	361 (100.00%)	540 (100.00%)	210 (100.00%)	750 (100.00%)

Table 3.10.12: Distribution of the Populations According to the Persons in Labour Force and Persons Actually Working

Persons in Labour Force and Actually Working	Population-I & II			Population-III			All Populations		
	M	F	T	M	F	T	M	F	T
Persons in Labour Force	96.48%	85.42%	90.82%	81.68%	25.47%	53.89%	45.14%	33.10%	78.24%
Persons in Actual Work	94.91%	81.87%	88.24%	75.09%	22.47%	49.07%	43.51%	31.40%	74.91%
Persons Above 14 Years	100.00%	100.00%	100.00%	100.00%	100.00%	100.00%	100.00%	100.00%	100.00%
No. of Persons above 14 Years	511	535	1046	273	267	540	784	802	1586

Table 3.10.13: Distribution of the Populations According to the Incidence of Unemployment

Persons Unemployed and in Labour Force	Population-I & II			Population-III			All Populations		
	M	F	T	M	F	T	M	F	T
Incidence of Unemployment	1.63%	4.16%	2.79%	8.07%	11.76%	8.93%	57.70%	42.30%	100.00%
Persons in Labour Force	100.00%	100.00%	100.00%	100.00%	100.00%	100.00%	100.00%	100.00%	100.00%
No. of Persons in Labour Force	493	457	950	223	68	291	716	525	1241

Table 3.10.14: Distribution of the Populations According to the Children in Labour Force and Children Actually Working

Children in Labour Force	Population-I & II			Population-III			All Populations		
and Actually Working	M	F	T	M	F	T	M	F	T
Children in Labour Force	90.59%	89.07%	89.86%	6.41%	5.00%	5.80%	40.24%	36.68%	76.92%
Children in Actual Work	86.01%	82.24%	84.19%	5.13%	5.00%	5.07%	38.13%	33.89%	72.02%
Total	100.00%	100.00%	100.00%	100.00%	100.00%	100.00%	100.00%	100.00%	100.00%
No. of Children	393	366	759	78	60	138	471	426	897

Table 3.10.15: Distribution of the Working Population According to the Working Children and Working Adults

Working Population	Population-I & II			Population-III			All Populations		
	M	F	T	M	F	T	M	F	T
Working Children	41.07%	40.73%	40.91%	1.91%	4.76%	2.57%	18.65%	16.58%	35.23%
Working Adults	58.93%	59.27%	59.09%	98.09%	95.24%	97.43%	37.62%	27.15%	64.77%
All Working Population	100.00%	100.00%	100.00%	100.00%	100.00%	100.00%	100.00%	100.00%	100.00%
No. of Working People	823	739	1562	209	63	272	1032	802	1834

Table 3.10.16: Distribution of Working Population According to the Types of Primary Occupation

Primary Occupation	Population-I			Population-II			Population-I & II			Population-III			All Populations		
	M	F	T	M	F	T	M	F	T	M	F	T	M	F	T
Type-A	0.98	0.39	1.37	1.24	0.00	1.24	1.15	0.13	1.28	31.99	5.15	37.13	5.73	0.87	6.60
Type-B	9.02	2.75	11.72	5.42	2.57	7.98	6.59	2.62	9.22	27.94	4.04	31.99	9.76	2.84	12.60
Type-C	17.06	18.63	35.68	17.11	19.39	36.50	17.09	19.14	36.24	14.34	13.60	27.94	16.68	18.32	35.00
Type-D	0.39	0.20	0.59	0.29	0.19	0.48	0.32	0.19	0.51	0.00	0.00	0.00	0.27	0.16	0.43
Type-E	26.47	24.12	50.59	28.04	25.76	53.80	27.53	25.22	52.75	0.37	0.00	0.37	23.50	21.48	44.98
Type-F	0.00	0.00	0.00	0.00	0.00	0.00	0.00	0.00	0.00	1.84	0.37	2.21	0.27	0.05	0.32
Working Population	53.92	46.08	100.00	52.09	47.91	100.00	52.69	47.31	100.00	76.84	23.16	100.00	56.27	43.73	100.00
No. of Working People	275	235	510	548	504	1052	823	739	1562	209	63	272	1032	802	1834

A - Salaried Workers of 'Traditional' Sector of the Economy.

B - Skilled Workers (*Mistris*), Handicraft Persons and Small Merchants.

C - Sellers of their Labour to People for the Personal Service and Consumption of the Buyers Instead of Using their Labour Power to obtain a Surplus Value.

D - Skin Sellers Exchanging their Surv val against the Possibility of Potential Destruction.

E - Urban Waste Recycle Workers.

F - Miscellaneous (Includes Pensioner and Landlord/landlady who survives on the rents).

Table 3.10.17: Distribution of the Households According to the Family Income Per Day

Level of Household Income Per Day	Households in Pop-I	Households in Pop-II	Households in Pop-I & II	Households Pop-III	Households All Pops.
Less than Rs. 50	26.26%	21.61%	23.15%	3.68%	18.00%
More than Rs. 50 but less than Rs. 75	57.54%	45.71%	49.63%	6.99%	38.27%
More than Rs. 75 but less than Rs. 100	11.17%	10.80%	10.93%	16.91%	14.00%
More than Rs. 100	5.03%	21.88%	16.30%	72.43%	29.73%
All Households	100.00%	100.00%	100.00%	100.00%	100.00%
No. of Households	179	361	540	210	750

Table 3.10.18: Distribution of the Households According to the Level of Monthly Savings

Level of Monthly Household Savings	Households in Pop-I	Households in Pop-II	Households in Pop-I & II	Households Pop-III	Households All Pops.
Non-existent	60.89%	61.22%	60.11%	16.19%	48.53%
Less than Rs. 100	9.50%	22.44%	17.22%	23.33%	18.93%
More than Rs. 100 but less than Rs. 200	15.64%	10.53%	12.22%	25.24%	15.87%
More than Rs. 200	13.97%	5.82%	8.52%	35.24%	16.67%
All Households	100.00%	100.00%	100.00%	100.00%	100.00%
No. of Households	179	361	540	210	750

Table 3.10.19: Distribution of the Child Labourers According to Age and Sex (Percentages)

Age Group	Child Labour in Population-I			Child Labour in Population-II			Child Labour in Population-I & II			Child Labour in Population-III			Child Labour in All Populations		
	M	F	T	M	F	T	M	F	T	M	F	T	M	F	T
5-9 years	23.62	20.06	43.69	27.58	26.36	53.94	25.67	23.32	48.98	0.00	0.00	0.00	25.39	23.07	48.46
10-14 years	30.74	25.57	56.31	23.94	22.12	46.06	27.23	23.79	51.02	57.14	42.86	100.00	27.55	23.99	50.64
All	54.37	45.93	100.00	51.52	48.48	100.00	52.90	47.10	100.00	57.14	42.86	100.00	52.94	47.06	100.00
No. of Child Labourer	168	141	309	170	160	330	338	301	639	4	3	7	342	304	646

Table 3.10.20: Distribution of the Child Labourers and the Children Populations According to Age and Sex (Percentages)

Age Group	Population-I			Population-II			Population-I & II			Population-III			All Populations		
	M	F	T	M	F	T	M	F	T	M	F	T	M	F	T
Child Labourers (5-9 years)	82.95	75.61	79.41	78.45	76.32	77.39	80.39	76.02	78.25	0.00	0.00	0.00	25.39	23.06	48.45
Total Children (5-9 years)	100.00	100.00	100.00	100.00	100.00	100.00	100.00	100.00	100.00	100.00	100.00	100.00	100.00	100.00	100.00
Total No. Children (5-9 years)	88	82	170	116	114	230	204	196	400	31	31	62	235	227	462
Child Labourers (10-14 years)	88.79	86.81	37.88	96.34	92.41	94.41	92.06	89.41	90.81	8.51	10.34	9.21	27.55	23.99	51.54
Total Children (10-14 years)	100.00	100.00	100.00	100.00	100.00	100.00	100.00	100.00	100.00	100.00	100.00	100.00	100.00	100.00	100.00
Total No. of Children (10-14 years)	107	91	198	82	79	161	189	170	359	47	29	76	236	199	435

Table 3.10.21: Distribution of the Child Labourers According to the Standard of Education (Percentages)

Educational Standard	Child Labourer in Population-I & II			Child Labourer in Population-III			Child Labourer in All Populations		
	M	F	T	M	F	T	M	F	T
Non-Literate	13.62	43.82	57.43	0.00	0.00	0.00	13.47	43.34	56.81
Can Sign Only	22.07	0.47	22.69	0.00	0.00	0.00	24.83	0.46	22.46
Class I to IV	12.68	2.66	15.34	14.29	42.86	57.14	12.69	3.10	15.79
Class V & Above	4.54	0.00	4.54	42.86	0.00	42.86	4.95	0.00	4.95
All	52.90	47.10	100.00	57.14	42.86	100.00	52.94	47.06	100.00
No. of Child Labourer	338	301	639	4	3	7	342	304	646

Table 3.10.22: Distribution of the Child Labourers According to the Years of Schooling (Percentages)

Educational Standard	Child Labourer in Population-I & II			Child Labourer in Population-III			Child Labourer in All Populations		
	M	F	T	M	F	T	M	F	T
None	13.62	43.82	57.43	0.00	0.00	0.00	13.47	43.34	56.81
One year to three years	30.20	1.72	31.92	14.29	42.86	57.14	30.03	2.17	32.20
More than three years	9.08	1.56	10.64	42.86	0.00	42.86	9.44	1.39	10.99
All	52.90	47.10	100.00	57.14	42.86	100.00	52.94	47.06	100.00
No. of Child Labourer	338	301	639	4	3	7	342	304	646

Table 3.10.23: Distribution of the Literate Child Labourers According to the Continuity of Study (Percentages)

Whether Continuing Study	Child Labourer in Population-I & II			Child Labourer in Population-III			Child Labourer in All Populations		
	M	F	T	M	F	T	M	F	T
No	51.10	3.68	54.78	14.29	28.56	42.86	50.18	4.30	54.48
Formal school	5.51	0.74	6.25	42.86	14.29	57.14	6.45	1.08	7.53
Non-formal school	35.66	3.31	38.97	0.00	0.00	0.00	34.77	3.23	37.99
All	92.28	7.72	100.00	57.15	42.85	100.00	91.40	8.60	100.00
No. of Literate Child Labourer	251	21	272	4	3	7	255	24	279

Table 3.10.24: Distribution of the Child Labourers According to the Main Reason for Leaving/ Not Sending to School (Percentages)

Main Reason for Leaving/Not Sending to School	Child Labourer in Population-I & II	Child Labourer in Population-III	Child Labourer in All Populations
Family needed contribution	34.88	33.33	38.87
Family could not afford to continue the study	37.98	0.00	37.76
Study became uninteresting	5.04	0.00	5.01
Apprenticeship to a skilled job more meaningful	3.90	66.67	3.66
Neeed money for own survival	18.80	0.00	18.69
All children either not literate or dropped out	100.00	100.00	100.00
No. of Children either not literate or dropped out	516	3	519

Table 3.10.25: Distribution of the Child Labourers According to the Status as Labourer

Type of Work	Child Labourer in Population-I & II			Child Labourer in Population-III			Child Labourer in All Populations		
	Male	Female	Total	Male	Female	Total	Male	Female	Total
Wage Earning	45.13%	36.31%	81.22%	28.57%	0.00%	42.86%	44.74%	35.91%	80.65%
Self Employed	4.28%	3.60%	7.98%	14.29%	0.00%	14.29%	4.49%	3.56%	8.05%
Household Business/ Occupation	3.60%	7.20%	10.80%	14.29%	42.86%	57.14%	3.72%	7.59%	11.30%
All	52.90%	47.10%	100.00%	57.14%	42.86%	100.00%	52.94%	47.06%	100.00%
No. of Child Labourer	338	301	639	4	3	7	342	304	646

Table 3.10.26: Distribution of the Child Labourers According to the Age of Entering Work

Type of Work	Child Labourer in Population-I & II			Child Labourer in Population-III			Child Labourer in All Populations		
	Male	Female	Total	Male	Female	Total	Male	Female	Total
Below 6 years	8.61%	11.58%	20.19%	0.00%	0.00%	0.00%	8.51%	11.45%	19.97%
6 years to 9 years	29.42%	11.74%	41.16%	14.29%	14.29%	28.57%	29.26%	11.76%	41.02%
10 years to 14 years	14.87%	23.79%	38.65%	42.86%	28.57%	71.43%	15.17%	23.84%	39.01%
All	52.90%	47.10%	100.00%	57.14%	42.86%	100.00%	52.94%	47.06%	100.00%
No. of Child Labourer	338	301	639	4	3	7	342	304	646

Table 3.10.27: Distribution of the Child Labourers According to the Working Hours Per Day

Working Hours per Day	Child Labourer in Population-I & II			Child Labourer in Population-III			Child Labourer in All Populations		
	Male	Female	Total	Male	Female	Total	Male	Female	Total
Less than 2 hours	4.07%	7.04%	11.11%	14.29%	0.00%	14.29%	4.18%	6.96%	11.14%
2 hours to 6 hours	5.01%	8.45%	13.46%	42.86%	28.57%	71.43%	5.42%	8.67%	14.09%
Above 6 hours	43.82%	31.46%	75.27%	0.00%	14.29%	14.29%	43.34%	31.42%	74.77%
Total	52.90%	47.10%	100.00%	57.14%	42.86%	100.00%	52.34%	47.06%	100.00%
No. of Child Labourer	338	301	639	4	3	7	342	304	646

Table 3.10.28: Distribution of the Child Labourers According to the Availability of Resting Time within the Working Hours

Resting Time	Child Labourer in Population-I & II			Child Labourer in Population-III			Child Labourer in All Populations		
	Male	Female	Total	Male	Female	Total	Male	Female	Total
Non-existent	21.13%	15.96%	37.09%	0.00%	0.00%	0.00%	20.90%	15.79%	36.69%
Less than 30 minutes	31.46%	29.58%	61.03%	14.29%	0.00%	14.29%	31.27%	29.26%	60.53%
30 minutes to one hour	0.31%	1.56%	1.88%	42.86%	42.86%	85.71%	0.77%	2.01%	2.79%
More than one hour	0.00%	0.00%	0.00%	0.00%	0.00%	0.00%	0.00%	0.00%	0.00%
All	52.90%	47.10%	100.00%	57.14%	42.86%	100.00%	52.94%	47.06%	100.00%
No. of Child Labourer	338	301	639	4	3	7	342	304	646

Table 3.10.29: Distribution of the Child Labourers According to the Number of Working Days in a Week

No. of Working Days in a Week	Child Labourer in Population-I & II			Child Labourer in Population-III			Child Labourer in All Populations		
	Male	Female	Total	Male	Female	Total	Male	Female	Total
7 days	13.77%	18.31%	32.08%	14.29%	28.57%	42.86%	13.78%	18.42%	32.20%
6 days	3.49%	26.13%	59.62%	42.86%	14.29%	57.14%	33.59%	26.01%	59.60%
5 days	1.56%	1.25%	2.82%	0.00%	0.00%	0.00%	1.55%	1.24%	2.79%
4 days	1.41%	0.63%	2.03%	0.00%	0.00%	0.00%	1.39%	0.62%	2.01%
3 days	0.94%	0.47%	1.41%	0.00%	0.00%	0.00%	0.93%	0.46%	1.39%
Less than 3 days	1.72%	0.31%	2.04%	0.00%	0.00%	0.00%	1.70%	0.31%	2.01%
All	52.90%	47.10%	100.00%	57.14%	42.86%	100.00%	52.94%	47.06%	100.00%
No. of Child Labourer	338	301	639	4	3	7	342	304	646

Table 3.10.30: Distribution of the Child Labourers According to the Type of Sector of the Economy They Work

Sector of the Economy	Child Labourer in Population-I & II			Child Labourer in Population-III			Child Labourer in All Populations		
	Male	Female	Total	Male	Female	Total	Male	Female	Total
Formal sector	0.63%	0.31%	0.94%	14.29%	0.00%	14.29%	0.77%	0.31%	1.08%
Informal sector	52.27%	46.79%	99.06%	42.86%	42.86%	85.71%	52.17%	46.75%	98.92%
All	52.90%	47.10%	100.00%	57.14%	42.86%	100.00%	52.94%	46.75%	100.00%
No. of Child Labourer	338	301	639	4	3	7	342	304	646

Table 3.10.31: Distribution of the Child Labourers According to the Type of Primary Occupation

Primary Occupation	Child Labourer in Population-I & II			Child Labourer in Population-III			Child Labourer in All Populations		
	Male	Female	Total	Male	Female	Total	Male	Female	Total
Workers of 'Traditional' Sector of the Economy (A)	0.94%	0.00%	0.94%	14.29%	0.00%	14.29%	1.08%	0.00%	1.08%
Skilled Workers (*Mistris*), Handicraft Persons and Small Merchants (B)	12.21%	0.94%	13.15%	28.57%	14.29%	42.86%	12.38%	1.08%	13.46%
Sellers of their Labour to People for the Personal Service and Consumption of the Buyers Instead of Using their Labour Power to Obtain a Surplus Value (C)	15.65%	26.91%	42.56%	14.29%	28.57%	42.86%	15.63%	26.94%	42.57%
Skin Sellers Exchanging their Survival Against the Possibility of Potential Destruction or Trade their Deterioration (D)	0.31%	0.00%	0.31%	0.00%	0.00%	0.00%	0.00%	0.31%	0.31%
Urban Waste Recycle Workers (E)	23.79%	19.25%	43.04%	0.00%	0.00%	0.00%	23.53%	19.04%	42.57%
All	52.90%	47.10%	100.00%	57.14%	42.86%	100.00%	52.94%	47.06%	100.00%
No. of Child Labourer	338	301	639	4	3	7	342	304	646

Table 3.10.32: Distribution of the Child Labourers According to the Primary Occupation (Details of Occupations) (Percentages)

Primary Occupation	Child Labourer in Population-I & II			Child Labourer in Population-III			Child Labourer in All Populations		
	Male	Female	Total	Male	Female	Total	Male	Female	Total
A Temporary	0.94	0.00	0.94	14.29	0.00	14.29	1.08	0.00	1.08
Permanent	0.00	0.00	0.00	0.00	0.00	0.00	0.00	0.00	0.00
B Apprentice to Skilled Worker, Handicraft Persons	11.58	0.94	12.52	14.29	14.29	28.58	11.61	1.08	12.69
Small Merchant	0.63	0.00	0.63	14.29	0.00	14.29	0.77	0.00	0.77
C Domestic Help	0.00	21.44	21.44	0.00	0.00	0.00	0.00	21.21	21.21
Porter	2.66	0.00	2.66	0.00	0.00	0.00	2.63	0.00	2.63
Van/Rickshaw Puller	2.35	0.00	2.35	0.00	0.00	0.00	2.32	0.00	2.32
Helper in Construction	1.88	1.11	2.97	0.00	0.00	0.00	1.86	1.08	2.94
Tea stall/Restaurant Worker	5.16	1.88	7.04	14.29	0.00	14.29	5.26	1.86	7.12
Helper in Transport	0.00	0.00	0.00	0.00	0.00	0.00	0.00	0.00	0.00
Shoe-shiner	0.93	1.10	2.03	0.00	0.00	0.00	0.93	1.08	2.01
Bidi Worker	1.41	0.94	2.35	0.00	0.00	0.00	1.39	0.93	2.32
Packet (*thonga*) Making	0.00	0.31	0.31	0.00	28.58	28.58	0.00	0.62	0.62
Other	1.25	0.16	1.41	0.00	0.00	0.00	1.24	0.15	1.39
D Beggar	0.31	0.00	0.31	0.00	0.00	0.00	0.31	0.00	0.31
Prostitute	0.00	0.00	0.00	0.00	0.00	0.00	0.00	0.00	0.00
Delinquent	0.00	0.00	0.00	0.00	0.00	0.00	0.00	0.00	0.00
E Scrap Picker	15.49	15.02	30.51	0.00	0.00	0.00	15.30	14.86	30.19
Scrap Buyer (door-to-door)	4.23	0.94	5.16	0.00	0.00	0.00	4.18	0.93	5.11
Scrap Sorter	4.07	3.29	7.36	0.00	0.00	0.00	4.02	3.25	7.27
Scrap Dealer	0.00	0.00	0.00	0.00	0.00	0.00	0.00	0.00	0.00
All	52.90	47.10	100.00	57.14	42.86	100.00	52.94	47.06	100.00
No. of Child Labourer	338	301	639	4	3	7	342	304	646

Table 3.10.33: Distribution of the Child Labourers According to the Nature of Work (Percentages)

Nature of Work	Child Labourer in Population-I & II			Child Labourer in Population-III			Child Labourer in All Populations		
	Male	Female	Total	Male	Female	Total	Male	Female	Total
Non-hazardous	38.50	37.87	76.37	57.14	42.86	100.00	38.70	37.93	76.63
Hazardous	14.40	9.23	23.63	0.00	0.00	0.00	14.24	9.13	23.37
All	52.90	47.10	100.00	57.14	42.86	100.00	52.94	47.06	100.00
No. of Child Labourer	338	301	636	4	3	7	342	304	646

Table 3.10.34: Distribution of the Child Labourers According to the Level of Daily Income (Percentages)

Level of Daily Income	Child Labourer in Population-I & II			Child Labourer in Population-III			Child Labourer in All Populations		
	Male	Female	Total	Male	Female	Total	Male	Female	Total
Less than Rs. 10	11.58	16.28	27.86	14.29	28.57	42.86	11.61	16.41	28.02
Rs. 10 to Rs. 24	20.19	18.94	39.12	0.00	0.00	0.00	19.97	18.73	38.70
Rs. 25 to Rs. 49	16.90	8.76	25.67	28.57	14.29	42.86	17.03	8.82	25.85
Rs. 50 or more	4.23	3.13	7.36	14.29	0.00	14.29	4.33	3.09	7.43
All	52.90	47.10	100.00	57.14	42.86	100.00	52.94	47.06	100.00
No. of Child Labourer	338	301	639	4	3	7	342	304	646

Table 3.10.35: Distribution of the Child Labourers According to the Distance of the Workplace (Percentages)

Distance of the Work Place	Child Labourer in Population-I & II			Child Labourer in Population-III			Child Labourer in All Populations		
	Male	Female	Total	Male	Female	Total	Male	Female	Total
Within one km	9.39	15.96	25.35	14.29	42.86	57.14	9.44	16.25	25.70
One km to Less than Five kms	34.59	27.07	61.66	42.86	0.00	42.86	34.67	26.78	61.45
Five kms and above	8.92	4.07	12.99	0.00	0.00	0.00	8.82	4.02	12.85
All	52.90	47.10	100.00	57.14	42.86	100.00	52.94	47.06	100.00
No. of Child Labourer	338	301	639	4	3	7	342	304	646

Table 3.10.36: Distribution of the Child Labourers According to the Mode of Transport to the Workplace (Percentages)

Principal Mode of Transport	Child Labourer in Population-I & II			Child Labourer in Population-III			Child Labourer in All Populations		
	Male	Female	Total	Male	Female	Total	Male	Female	Total
Not Required	10.95	20.50	31.46	28.57	42.86	71.43	11.14	20.74	31.89
Required but do not Afford/Avail	26.45	20.03	46.48	0.00	0.00	0.00	26.16	19.82	45.97
By Bus	13.30	6.57	19.87	28.57	0.00	28.57	13.47	6.50	19.97
By Train—Without Ticket	1.41	0.00	0.00	0.00	0.00	0.00	1.39	0.00	1.39
By Train—With Ticket	0.78	0.00	0.00	0.00	0.00	0.00	0.77	0.00	0.77
All	52.90	47.10	100.00	57.14	42.86	100.00	52.94	47.06	100.00
No. of Child Labourer	338	301	639	4	3	7	342	304	646

Table 3.10.37: Distribution of the Child Labourers According to the Part of Earning Spent on Transport to the Workplace (Percentages)

Part of the Earning Spend	Child Labourer in Population-I & II			Child Labourer in Population-III			Child Labourer in All Populations		
	Male	Female	Total	Male	Female	Total	Male	Female	Total
None	37.40	40.53	77.93	28.57	42.86	71.43	37.31	40.56	77.87
Less than 10 per cent	10.33	4.54	14.87	0.00	0.00	0.00	10.22	4.49	14.70
10 per cent to 25 per cent	4.23	1.25	5.48	28.57	0.00	28.57	4.49	1.24	5.73
More than 25 per cent	0.94	0.78	1.72	0.00	0.00	0.00	0.93	0.77	1.70
All	52.90	47.10	100.00	57.14	42.86	100.00	100.00	47.06	100.00
No. of Child Labourer	338	301	639	4	3	7	342	304	646

Table 3.10.38: Distribution of the Child Labourers According to the Time Spent to Travel to the Workplace (Percentages)

Time Spend to Reach the Work Place	Child Labourer in Population-I & II			Child Labourer in Population-III			Child Labourer in All Populations		
	Male	Female	Total	Male	Female	Total	Male	Female	Total
None or Nominal	9.23	15.96	25.20	28.57	42.86	71.43	9.44	16.25	25.70
Less than 30 minutes	30.67	25.20	55.87	28.57	0.00	28.57	30.65	24.92	55.57
30 minutes to less than one hour	12.21	5.63	17.84	0.00	0.00	0.00	12.07	5.57	17.65
More than one hour	0.78	0.31	1.10	0.00	0.00	0.00	0.77	0.31	1.08
All	52.90	47.10	100.00	57.14	42.86	100.00	52.94	47.06	100.00
No. of Child Labourer	338	301	639	4	3	7	342	304	646

Table 3.10.39: Distribution of the Child Labourers According to the Facilities Available at the Workplaces (Percentages)

Facilities Available		Child Labourer in Population-I & II	Child Labourer in Population-III	Child Labourer in All Populations
Hazard prevention measures	Adequate	0.00	0.00	0.00
	Inadequate	8.61	0.00	8.51
	Absent	15.02	0.00	14.86
	Not required	76.37	100.00	76.63
Self-protection measures	Adequate	0.00	0.00	0.00
	Inadequate	2.03	0.00	2.01
	Absent	21.60	0.00	21.36
	Not required	76.37	100.00	76.63
First aid facilities	Adequate	0.00	0.00	0.00
	Inadequate	8.45	42.86	8.82
	Absent	86.85	57.14	91.18
	Not required	0.00	0.00	0.00
Toilet facilities	Adequate	0.00	0.00	0.00
	Inadequate	34.90	28.57	34.83
	Absent	65.10	71.43	65.17
	Not required	0.00	0.00	0.00
No. of Child Labourer		639 (100.00)	7 (100.00)	646 (100.00)

Table 3.10.40: Distribution of the Child Labourers According to the Number of Accidents Happened in Working Life

No. of Accidents Happened in the Working Life	Child Labourer in Population-I & II	Child Labourer in Population-III	Child Labourer in All Populations
Never	17.68%	100.00%	18.57%
Only Once	28.01%	0.00%	27.71%
Two to Five Times	44.76%	0.00%	44.27%
More than Five Times	9.55%	0.00%	9.44%
All	100.00%	100.00%	100.00%
No. of Child Labourer	639	7	646

Table 3.10.41: Distribution of Wage-Earning Child Labourers According to the Number of Employees Present in the Working Unit

Number of Employees Present in the Working Unit	Wage-Earning Child Labourer in Population-I & II	Wage-Earning Child Labourer in Population-III	Wage-Earning Child Labourer in All Populations
Less than five	36.30%	50.00%	36.35%
Five to ten	51.65%	50.00%	51.65%
More than ten	12.04%	0.00%	12.00%
All Wage-Earning Child Labourers	100.00%	100.00%	100.00%
No. of Wage-Earning Child Labourer	573	2	575

Table 3.10.42: Distribution of Wage-Earning Child Labourers According to the Recipients of the Wage

Recipient of the Wage	Wage-Earning Child Labourer in Population-I & II			Wage-Earning Child Labourer in Population-III			Wage-Earning Child Labourer in All Populations		
	Male	Female	Total	Male	Female	Total	Male	Female	Total
Self	31.24%	14.66%	45.90%	100.00%	0.00%	100.00%	31.40%	14.61%	46.09%
Father	11.69%	8.90%	20.59%	0.00%	0.00%	0.00%	11.65%	8.87%	20.52%
Mother	1.40%	3.66%	5.06%	0.00%	0.00%	0.00%	1.39%	3.65%	5.04%
Other Elder member of the Family	7.33%	14.83%	22.16%	0.00%	0.00%	0.00%	7.30%	14.78%	22.08%
Others	4.01%	2.27%	6.28%	0.00%	0.00%	0.00%	4.00%	2.26%	6.26%
All	55.67%	44.33%	100.00%	100.00%	0.00%	100.00%	55.83%	44.17%	100.00%
No. of Wage-Earning Child Labourer	319	254	573	2	0	2	321	274	575

Table 3.10.43: Distribution of Wage-Earning Child Labourers According to the Type of the Fellow Employees' Behaviour in the Workplace

Type of Behaviour	Wage Earning Child Labourer in Population-I & II			Wage Earning Child Labourer in Population-III			Wage Earning Child Labourer in All Populations		
	Male	Female	Total	Male	Female	Total	Male	Female	Total
Frequently Harsh	14.66%	8.38%	23.04%	0.00%	0.00%	0.00%	14.61%	8.35%	22.96%
Occasionally Harsh	39.09%	33.86%	72.95%	100.00%	0.00%	100.00%	39.30%	33.74%	73.04%
Not Harsh	1.92%	2.09%	4.01%	0.00%	0.00%	0.00%	1.91%	2.09%	4.00%
All	55.67%	44.33%	100.00%	100.00%	0.00%	100.00%	55.83%	44.17%	100.00%
No. of Wage-Earning Child Labourer	319	254	573	2	0	2	321	254	575

Table 3.10.44: Distribution of Wage-Earning Child Labourers According to the Type of Employer's Behaviour in the Workplace

Type of Behaviour	Wage-Earning Child Labourer in Population-I & II			Wage-Earning Child Labourer in Population-III			Wage-Earning Child Labourer in All Populations		
	Male	Female	Total	Male	Female	Total	Male	Female	Total
Frequently harsh	14.66%	8.38%	23.04%	0.00%	0.00%	0.00%	14.61%	8.35%	22.96%
Occasionally harsh	39.09%	33.86%	72.95%	100.00%	0.00%	100.00%	39.30%	33.74%	73.04%
Not harsh	1.92%	2.09%	4.01%	0.00%	0.00%	0.00%	1.91%	2.09%	4.00%
All	55.67%	44.33%	100.00%	100.00%	0.00%	100.00%	55.83%	44.17%	100.00%
No. of Wage-Earning Child Labourer	319	254	573	2	0	2	321	254	575

Table 3.10.45: Distribution of the Child Labourers According to the Mode of Receiving Wage or Income

Mode of Receiving Wage/Income	Child Labourer in Population-I & II	Child Labourer in Population-III	Child Labourer in All Populations
Daily	27.23%	0.00%	26.93%
Weekly	54.15%	42.86%	54.02%
Monthly	7.20%	0.00%	7.12%
Not Applicable	11.42%	57.14%	11.92%
All	100.00%	100.00%	100.00%
No. of Child Labourer	639	7	646

Table 3.10.46: Distribution of the Child Labourers According to the Presence or Absence of Family

Presence or Absence of Family	Child Labourer in Population-I & II	Child Labourer in Population-III	Child Labourer in All Populations
Present	100.00%	100.00%	100.00%
Absent	0.00%	0.00%	0.00%
All	100.00%	100.00%	100.00%
No. of Child Labourer	639	7	646

Table 3.10.47: Distribution of the Child Labourers According to the Contribution of His/Her Income to the Household

Part of His/Her Contribution to Household	Child Labourer in Population-I & II	Child Labourer in Population-III	Child Labourer in All Populations
None	4.85%	0.00%	4.80%
Less than ten per cent of the Earning	11.42%	14.29%	18.42%
Ten to fifty per cent of the Earning	18.47%	0.00%	11.30%
More than fifty per cent of the Earning	65.26%	85.71%	65.48%
Total	100.00%	100.00%	100.00%
No. of Child Labourer	639	7	646

Table 3.10.48: Distribution of the Child Labourers According to the Level of Dependence of the Household on His/Her Income

Level of Dependence	Child Labourer in Population-I & II	Child Labourer in Population-III	Child Labourer in All Populations
None	4.85%	0.00%	4.80%
Nominal	23.32%	42.86%	23.53%
Substantial	71.05%	57.14%	71.21%
Complete	0.47%	0.00%	0.46%
All	100.00%	100.00%	100.00%
No. of Child Labourer	639	7	646

Table 3.10.49: Distribution of the Child Labourers According to the Level of His/Her Own Spending from His/Her Earning

Level of Own Spending from His/Her Earning	Child Labourer in Population-I & II	Child Labourer in Population-III	Child Labourer in All Populations
Less than ten per cent of Earning	60.88%	28.57%	60.53%
Ten per cent to fifty per cent of Earning	14.40%	71.43%	15.01%
More than fifty per cent of Earning	19.87%	0.00%	19.66%
Entire Earning	4.85%	0.00%	4.80%
All	100.00%	100.00%	100.00%
No. of Child Labourer	639	7	646

Table 3.10.50: Distribution of the Child Labourers According to the Frequency of Leaving Job

Number of Times of Leaving Job	Child Labourer in Population-I & II	Child Labourer in Population-III	Child Labourer in All Populations
Never	44.76%	57.14%	44.89%
Once	34.59%	28.57%	34.52%
Two to five times	14.08%	14.29%	14.09%
More than five times	6.57%	0.00%	6.50%
All	100.00%	100.00%	100.00%
No. of Child Labourer	639	7	646

Table 3.10.51: Distribution of the Child Labourers According to the Reason for Leaving Job

Reason for Leaving Job	Child Labourer in Population-I & II	Child Labourer in Population-III	Child Labourer in All Populations
Never left the job since his/her absorbtion	44.76%	57.14%	44.89%
Very low pay	13.46%	42.86%	13.78%
Intolerable working condition	15.02%	0.00%	14.86%
Accident-prone job	11.42%	0.00%	11.30%
Learning a skilled and more lucrative job	3.13%	0.00%	3.10%
Fired/Terminated	8.29%	0.00%	8.20%
Too much distance to the workplace	2.66%	0.00%	2.63%
Other reasons	1.25%	0.00%	1.24%
All	100.00%	100.00%	100.00%
No. of Child Labourer	639	7	646

4

Child Labour in a Third World Urban Situation: Towards a Conclusion

This study on the child labour situation in Kolkata opened a discursive space where one can see an intricate interplay of globalisation, marginalisation of population and the problem of child labour. The study started during the early years of 1990s when India was entering into the bandwagon of WTO and the fieldwork was continued for over a decade witnessing the effect of the 'successful' integration of Indian economy with the world economy. Worldwide trends indicated that during this period footloose capital freely travelled from one the developed nations to the developing world but the labour force mostly remained confined within the national boundaries. Cities became the destination of capital particularly in Third World leading to a huge demographic transition to the main urban centres of the country. The loss of livelihood in the rural areas due to various SAP-related measures also formed another major reason for this demographic transformation. It has been predicted that half of the Third World population will have to live in the cities by 2020 and about 60 cities, most of them are in Third World, will have 5 million plus people. Megacities in the Third World like Mexico City, Mumbai, Lagos, Dhaka, Karachi and Kolkata will have a population of more than 20 million.

The author argued that most of the observable effects of globalisation happened in the Third World cities and the dominant views on urban life, mostly formed by the observers from North. These views are already facing challenges as they could not adequately explain various Third World urban phenomena. Child labour in Third World cities is one such phenomenon that eluded Western observers from grappling the ground realities in its entirety. Correlations have been frequently drawn between the child labour and globalisation as International Labour Organisation (ILO) found a steep increase in magnitude of child labour with the advent of globalisation. Anthropologists with their techniques of intensive ethnographic fieldwork would be better positioned for these studies which might help in creating Third Worldly understanding of the problem of child labour.

CHILD LABOUR IN THE THIRD WORLD

Though the observers vary widely on the conceptions and the main determinants of child labour it has been widely accepted that the work impairs the health and development of children can be regarded as child labour. It means a denial of the right of education and of the opportunity to reach full physical and psychological development (ILO, 1996: 8). Thus the child labourers are the children under 14 years of age working mainly in the informal sectors, in conditions harmful or potentially harmful to the children, underpaid for their work and are subjected to other forms of exploitation. According to some observers any child between the age of 5 and 14 years and out of school should be treated as a working child and it is the duty of the state to provide universal education for its citizens without which it is not possible to combat a problem like child labour. Other observers believe in more gradual approach which is a combination of prohibition and regulation i.e. banning child labour from the hazardous occupations and regulating as well as gradual withdrawal of child labour from the non-hazardous occupations. Some other observers believe that the state must create appropriate infrastructure for a motivating and gainful educational system for the children that would be interesting to both the parents as well as their children. Since it is the household which decides on the allocation of a child's time between leisure, schooling, household activities and employment more household level studies are necessary to properly understand the main determinants of child labour. But households are not the 'stand-alone' entities in determining the fate of a child as there are other important factors beyond the direct control of the households like the level of marginality of the family, schooling environment, the demand for child labour, the cultural understanding of child labour in that society, etc. must be simultaneously considered to understand the problem properly.

Observers also differ on the magnitude of the problem of child labour. According to ILO there are at least 120 million children who work full-time and another 130 million who are involved in part-time work. Most of these children are from the Third World countries. Indian government has been repeatedly accused of suppressing the number of its child labour population as the 2001 census puts the figure to over 12 million while observers believe that a much higher number of children work full-time in India.

The major child labour intensive occupations in India include in the sectors of match and fireworks in Sivakasi, stone-quarries in Kerala, Andhra and Madhya Pradesh, mines in Meghalaya, fishing in Kerala, handlooms in Tamil Nadu, lock-making in Uttar Pradesh, carpet weaving in Jammu and Kashmir and Uttar Pradesh, pottery-making in Kashmir and Uttar Pradesh, glass factories in Uttar Pradesh, gem polishing in Rajasthan, *beedi*-making in Andhra, Tamil Nadu, and Gujarat, brassware industry in Uttar Pradesh, diamond industry in Gujarat, and leather units in Uttar Pradesh, Madhya Pradesh and Rajasthan.

Some observers believe that the situation of child labour has actually worsened in the Third World cities primarily due to SAP-related measures. The wide-ranging insecurity has prevailed over the vulnerable section of population and it has been multiplied with the advent of globalisation. During this work, the author found this increased insecurity among the marginalised population in the city of Kolkata as the local government was compelled to take city development Programmes without giving any tangible alternative to the affected people and the problem of the proliferation of child labour can be related with this insecurity.

THE RESEARCH DESIGN AND THE FINDINGS

The third chapter of this book has dealt with the research design employed to conduct the research and the details of the findings from the field. In the first section dealing with the research design the author briefly discussed how anthropologists became a little late entrant in taking up the burning urban issues like urban poverty, urban marginalisation, ethnic tension in a city, urban communal violence, etc. and when the anthropologists took up urban issues for study they continued to focus on their traditional target groups i.e. tribal and peasant people in the urban areas until recently. This trend got somewhat changed from late 1960s with the arrival of various urban ethnographic studies. The studies by Elliot Liebow (1967) on the marginalised people in urban areas and more recently Philippe Bourgois's account of street culture in East Harlem (1995) were two such highpoints in urban ethnographic studies.

At the empirical level, the author studied three different settlements (Population-I, Population-II and Population-III) in the city of Kolkata. Population-I and Population-II were squatter settlements and the inhabitants were living without any security of tenure. These two populations were termed as Control Group in this study and both the settlements were eventually destroyed to implement city development programmes. Population-III was a recognised slum where the inhabitants lived with a kind of security of tenure with the enactment of 'Calcutta *Thika* and Other Tenancies and Lands (Acquisition and Regulation) Act, 1981' under which they could live and build houses on their land but they could not legally sell those. The author considered this population as the Programme Group since it received a Programme in the form of security of tenure for a long time.

Research design also included the standard anthropological fieldwork techniques which were employed during this fieldwork. Thus the formal training in anthropology had helped the author in gaining entry in the fieldsites, rapport building and selection of informants. The author extensively used both the non-participant observation and the participant observation as principal methods of data collection along with semi-structure interviewing. Along with these techniques the author used free lists and ranking during this fieldwork to determine and rank the socially cognisant items among the people under study. Case study was also used frequently during this fieldwork to get detailed information on different aspects of the problem.

After discussing the research design the author made elaborative discussions on the results and analyses of the data collected from the actual fieldwork which would be most important for developing a Third Worldly understanding of this problem.

(a) Population Profiles

The population distribution according to age and sex showed that in the Control Group there were more people aged under 15 years indicating a higher birth rate than the Programme Group. Child woman ratios of both 0-4 years and 5-9 age groups showed a much higher proportion of children per woman in reproductive age in the Control Group in contrast to the Programme Group which again indicated an improved birth rate in the Programme Group.

(b) Educational Aspects of the Two Populations

Distribution of the educational standard has shown that more than half of the Control Group were either non-literates or could sign their names only and a very negligible proportion of this population had actually crossed the secondary education level, whereas none had gone beyond that level. People in the Programme Group, on the other hand, were much better positioned in this regard with fewer non-literate people, fewer people who can only sign their names and more people with higher level of education having passed the secondary and higher secondary levels. Few persons in the Programme Group even reached and/or passed the graduation level of education. Accordingly, the literacy rate in the Control Group was nearly 44 per cent and in the Programme Group this rate was much higher to nearly 79 per cent again indicating much better educational position in the Programme Group. Quite expectedly, the child literacy rate in the Control Group was much lower to nearly 47 per cent and the trend was even lower among the girls, which was caused due to a general lower status of women. The author made a detailed study on one such case Farah, a 10 years old girl from Population-I, discontinued her study due to various domestic and financial constraints. In the Programme Group the child literacy rate was as high as 95 per cent indicating that the newer generation including the girls in the Programme Group were getting more and more exposed to better educational scopes. This trend became quite visible when the author studied the case of Sikha Adhikary, an 11 years old girl from the Programme Group, who was still continuing her study in a nearby school.

(c) Contrasting Condition of Urban Marginality among the Two Groups

Next important issue is the condition of urban marginality of both the groups of people particularly in terms of their stay in the city of Kolkata. The author found that the majority of the residents of the Control Group recorded Bangladesh as their place of birth while significant proportions of them were born in Bihar as well as Jharkhand, and Kolkata. In the Programme Group as many as 73 per cent of the residents were born in Kolkata which was followed by the places in the adjoining districts of West Bengal and in Bangladesh.

In the city of Kolkata possessing ration card for the public distribution system happened to be one of the most important criteria of legitimacy of a settler in the city of Kolkata particularly for the marginalised section of the population since they required a valid permanent address to have a ration card. In the Control Group almost none of the settlers had any ration card as they did not have any valid permanent address. The few individuals who possessed the ration card in the Control Group registered their addresses at some other places. In the Programme Group all the eligible inhabitants had their own ration cards since these slum dwellers had legitimised permanent addresses. On the other hand, most of the eligible voters in the Control Group were registered in the electoral roll and quite expectedly the situation in Programme Group was quite similar. Thus despite being the legitimate voters the people in the Control Group were not regarded as the legitimate dwellers of the city and got evicted.

The distribution of the population according to the presence or absence of some indicators of collective consumption showed that the households in both the Control Group and the Programme Group were enjoying the facility of the presence of accessible primary school within 1 km of their households. But people in the Control Group did not have facilities like the presence of accessible hospital/health centre within 1 km, presence of *pucca* arterial road within settlement, presence of garbage disposal system, presence of planned drainage system, presence of legally obtained electricity, presence of separate family bathroom and presence of own tap as a source of drinking water. On the other hand, these facilities were present for the people in the Programme Group. Waterlogging during the rainy season was very common in both the settlements. Most households in the Control Group did not have fully water impermeable roofs, walls and floors whereas in the Programme Group almost all the houses were with water impermeable roofs, walls and floors. Separate ventilations and separate kitchens were present in majority of the houses in the Programme Group but very few families in the Control Group had these facilities.

(d) Economic Condition of the Two Groups

The author found that in the Control Group more people participated in work as the non-participation in work might mean starvation to these people which indicated a subsistence nature of the economy of this group of people. In the Programme Group lesser proportion of people actually participated in work as most of the children and women did not participate in the labour force. Similar picture was evident in the incidents of unemployment as less than 3 per cent in the labour force in the Control Group were unemployed whereas in the Programme Group less than 9 per cent of the total persons in the labour force were unemployed. Nearly 90 per cent of the children in the Control Group were working whereas in the Programme Group less than 6 per cent were working indicating a marked improvement in the attitude of the parents towards their children. In a similar vein, the author found that in the Control Group 40 per cent of the working population were children and in the Programme Group only two and half per cent of the working population were children during the time of this fieldwork.

Distribution of the type of primary occupations present among these marginalised people showed that during this fieldwork more than half of the working people in the Control Group was working as urban waste recycle workers (Type-E) followed by the sellers of their labour to people for the personal service and consumption of the buyers instead of using their labour power to obtain a surplus value (Type-C) and skilled workers (*mistris*), handicraft persons as well as small merchants (Type-B). There were very few persons (less than 2 per cent of the working population) in the Control Group who were salaried workers of traditional sector of economy (Type-A). It would also be worthwhile to note here that the skin sellers exchanging their survival against the possibility of potential destruction (e.g. prostitute, delinquent, etc.) or trade their deterioration (e.g. beggar) (Type-D) constituted a very negligible proportion (less than half per cent). This profession may be common among some other groups of marginalised people in the Third World urban areas but it was reported to be present in a very negligibly proportion in the Control Group. In the Programme Group, on the contrary, one can find as high as 37 per cent people were engaged in Type-A occupations in the traditional sector, closely followed by the proportion of population engaged in Type-B occupations as skilled workers etc. and Type-C occupations as sellers of their labour etc. None were engaged in Type-D occupation as skin sellers etc. and only one person was working in Type-E occupations as urban waste recycle workers.

The author observed during his fieldwork that in the Control Group nearly half of households had an income per day ranging between Rs. 51 and Rs. 75 and more than 23 per cent households earned less than Rs. 50. Nearly 11 per cent families in the Control Group earned more than Rs. 100 per day which could be considered as a decent level of income considering the prevalent economic situation of these people. In the Programme Group (where most of the earnings were on monthly basis and for this purpose those monthly incomes were converted to daily incomes) most households (nearly 77 per cent) had incomes over Rs. 100 per day and very few households (less than 4 per cent) earn less than Rs. 50 per day. Thus households in the Programme Group were much better-off than the Control Group as far as the level of income was concerned. In conformity with his earlier findings on income the author found that in majority of the cases (nearly 61 per cent) the level of monthly savings in the Control Group was non-existent and rest had a very small monthly savings ranging from less than Rs. 100 to Rs. 200, while a very few households had monthly savings over Rs. 200. In the Programme Group most of the families had a monthly savings of more than Rs. 200 and there were significant proportions of households in the Programme Group had little or no monthly savings. This would indicate that the expenditures in these households in the Programme Group were also high and these people were spending more than their incomes leading to the indebtedness in some families in this population.

(e) Child Labour Profile

The distribution of child labourers according to age and sex showed that more than half of them were from the age group of 10-14 years and the frequency of boys was slightly higher than the girls. It was also observed that in the Programme Group child labourers constituted less than 1 per cent of the total population—a remarkably improved scenario. It was also observed that more than 3/4th of the children between 5-9 years age and more than 90 per cent of the children between 10-14 years of age were working. However, in the Programme Group on 9 per cent of the children between 10-14 years of age were working while none in the age group of 5-9 years were working.

(f) Educational Scenario of the Child Labourers

The standard of education among the child labourers in All Populations as well as in the Control Group was very poor as nearly 80 per cent of them were either non-literate or could sign their names only whereas in the Programme Group all the child labourers were literate. Distribution of the child labourers according to the years of schooling showed that in All Populations as well as in the Control Group only 10 per cent child labourers had spent more than three years in school and nearly 30 per cent had spent between one to three years. In the Programme Group nearly 43 per cent child labourers had spent more than three years of schooling and rest had spent between one to three years of schooling. The picture regarding the distribution of child labourers according the continuity of study has reflected similar reality that more than 50 per cent of the child labourers had discontinued their study while most of the remaining child labourers (nearly 39 per cent) were continuing, though not always regularly, their education in the non-formal schools. In the Programme Group more than half of the child labourers were still continuing their study in the formal school during the time of this fieldwork but the rest discontinued their study. This study also investigated the main reasons for leaving/not sending the child labourers to school. In All Populations as well as in the Control Group the main reasons for drop-out were either family's need for more contributions from those children (nearly 35 per cent) or family could not afford to continue their study (nearly 38 per cent). Significant proportion of such discontinuations was caused by a need for money for the child labourer's own survival or due to the uninteresting study curricula. In the Programme Group, on the other hand, joining work for an apprenticeship to a financially lucrative occupation was the main cause of discontinuation of study.

(g) Economic Profile of the Child Labourers

To start with, the distribution of the type of work of child labourers showed that in All Populations as well as in the Control Group more than 80 per cent child labourers were wage earners and only few of them were engaged in household businesses/occupations or self-employed. In the Programme Group, however, most of the child labourers were engaged in household businesses/occupations. No remarkable gender specific trend was visible in this regard except the fact that the girls were more employed in the household businesses/occupations and lesser in the wage-earning occupation. The most frequent age of entering in work among these child labourers in All Populations as well as in the Control Group was between the ages of 6 years and 9 years and in the Programme Group the age of entering work among were between 10 years and 14 years. Working hours of the majority of child labourers (75 per cent) in All Populations as well as in the Control Group were above 6 hours whereas in the Programme Group majority of the child labourers were working between 2 hours and 6 hours. It was further observed during this fieldwork that most of the child labourers in All Populations as well as in the Control Group were allowed have less than 30 minutes of resting time within work hours whereas in the Programme Group almost all the child labourers were getting a resting time between 30 minutes to one hour. It was also evident that nearly 60 per cent of the child labourers in All Populations as well as in the Control Group had 6 working days in a week and many of these child labourers even worked in all 7 days in a week. In the Programme Group, a similar trend was visible indicating the desperate situation of the respective families even in this population which was otherwise much better-off compared to the Control Group.

Quite expectedly the author found during his fieldwork that almost all the child labourers were working in the informal sector of economy. If one looks at the type of primary occupation of these child labourers, one can find that most of the child labourers were either engaged in Type-E occupations of urban waste recycle workers or Type-C occupations of sellers of their labour, followed by Type-B occupations i.e. apprenticeship to the skilled work. In the Programme Group most of the child labourers were either engaged in Type-B occupations or Type-C occupations. If the details of these primary occupations were taken into account, one could again find that most of the child labourers were engaged in Type-E occupations as scrap pickers and in Type-C occupations as domestic helps. In All Populations as well as in the Control Group the child labourers were also frequently engaged as scrap sorters, door-to-door scrap buyers, tea stall/restaurant workers, helpers in construction, porters, van/rickshaw pullers, *beedi* workers, shoe-shiners, and *thonga* (paper packet) makers. In the Programme Group child labourers were most frequently engaged in Type-C occupations and Type-B occupations. None of the child labourers in this settlement were engaged in Type-D and Type-E occupations. Most of these child labourers in the Programme Group were engaged as *thonga* makers, tea stall/ restaurant workers or apprentices to skilled workers/handicraft persons. Another important observation in this work was that as many as 23 per cent of these child labourers, all of them from the Control Group, were engaged in hazardous nature of work. The level of daily income of these child labourers mostly varied between Rs. 10 and Rs. 25. Few (28 per cent) of them were earning less than Rs. 10 per day while some of them (nearly 26 per cent) were earning between Rs. 25 and Rs. 50. The daily earnings of a few (7 per cent) used to exceed Rs. 50 per day. In the Programme Group most of the child labourers were earning either less than Rs. 10 per day or between Rs. 25 and Rs. 50 per day.

Distance of the workplace of a child labourer in All Populations as well as in the Control Group in most cases varied between one km and five kms and in some cases it was within one km from the household. In the Programme Group the distances of the workplaces in most cases were within one km followed by the distances between one km and five kms. Mode of transport of the child labourers to reach their workplaces in most cases were non-existent as they preferred to walk the distance even if some mode of transport were required due to their financial constraints. In some cases they took buses or trains to reach their workplaces. In the Programme Group it was found that a majority of the child labourers walked the distance to their workplaces. During this fieldwork the author found that the child labourers in all three settlements were mostly spending nothing or very little (10 to 25 per cent) of their earnings in transport to the workplaces. The time spent to travel to the workplace in majority of cases was nominal or less than 30 minutes for these child labourers in both the Control Group and the Programme Group.

The author also studied the availability of the facilities which should be available at any workplace involving children in work. These include hazard prevention, self-protection mechanisms, first aid facilities and toilet facilities. Among the child labourers working in hazardous conditions in All Populations as well as in the Control Group the hazard prevention mechanisms were either inadequate or absent. In the Programme Group none of the child labourers were working in hazardous condition. Self-protection measures were also either inadequate or absent in the workplaces where the child labourers were employed. First aid facilities in all the workplaces of these child labourers were either absent or inadequate. Similar situation prevailed for the toilet facilities in the workplaces. In All Populations as well as in the Control Group it was found that most of the child labourers had experienced accidents of various kinds for two to five times in their working life even if they had not been working in the hazardous conditions. But in the Programme Group the child labourers had never faced accidents of any sort in their workplaces during their working life.

Wage earning child labourers, in most cases, were engaged in the working units where the number of employees ranged from five to ten. These wage-earning child labourers were mostly the recipients of their own wages although in some cases their father or some other elder member of the family received the wages on behalf of the child labourers. The type of behaviour met from the fellow adult employees in the workplaces by the child labourers in most cases were categorised as either occasionally harsh or frequently harsh. Similar types of behaviour were experienced by the child labourers from the employer in the workplaces. In most occasions, child labourers in both the Control Group and the Programme Group received wage or income on weekly basis.

All the child labourers presently studied had a family with which they were living. The contribution of the child labourer to his/her family in more than 65 per cent cases was more than half of its total earning. Sizable section of these child labourers used to contribute between ten to fifty per cent or less than ten per cent or nothing from their earnings. It would also be interesting to note that the level of dependence of the households on the child labourers' income in more than 71 per cent cases were substantial and in the rest the dependence were nominal or none. There were very few (less than half per cent) cases where this dependence was complete. Level of spending of the child labourers from his/her earnings in most cases did not cross the ten per cent mark of their earnings but there were significant number of cases where the child labourers used to spend more than 50 per cent of their earnings. If we look at the frequency of leaving job of the child labourers, we can find that the overwhelming proportion of them either had never left their jobs or left just once in their working life. Approximately one-fifth of the child labourers studied changed jobs from two to five times or more than five times. The reason for leaving job by these child labourers in most cases were intolerable working conditions or very low pay or accident-proneness of the job or were fired from the job.

(h) Thick Description of the Key Behaviours

Thick descriptions of the key behaviours were also tried during this study along with some thickly described case studies to understand the "webs of significance" which these people had woven within their cultural context. These thick descriptions contain some directly quoted interjections from the informants or direct reproductions of the fieldnotes to make it more translucent. One of the key observations was the attitude of parents towards their children. These attitudes were also quite different in the Control Group when compared with the findings from the Programme Group. In the Control Group, on the one hand, the author found several examples of beating the children on trivial issues, toddlers playing in dirty conditions, children defecating on the open space, boys getting preferential treatments compared to the girls, working children getting more preferences over the non-working children in the same family etc. Almost all these behaviours indicated that the children (particularly the girl children) were not seen as the future treasures in the Control Group. In the Programme Group, on the other hand, children (both boys and girls) were much better looked after as their education was considered important among these people with all the above unfavourable practices for the children were either not frequent or completely absent in the Programme Group. During this fieldwork, the author found that in the Control Group people spent most of their leisure times outside their houses and the common forms of recreational activities among these people were listening to music and chatting with each other. Younger generation in the Control Group was more attracted to the activities like colourful dresses, watching movies, fast-foods, etc. In the Programme Group, the author found that activities like chatting outside the house or listening to music were present but less frequently. But similar trends like wearing colourful dresses, watching movies, fast-foods, etc. were also frequent among the younger people.

The author also made observations on the world of perceptions of the child labourers which showed that most of the child labourers thought family's financial inability to continue to study as the main reason for their working. Parents' perceptions regarding their own children being child labourers were also dominated by the reasons like the family's inability to continue to child's study or need to learn job as an apprentice to a skilled work being a better prospect for their children. The author further observed that most employers considered that they employed the children in their establishments only to help the distressed families of those children. It was also observed during this fieldwork that most frequent leisure time activity of the child labourers was listening to radio but the most preferred recreational activity among these child labourers was watching movies in the television or in the theatres. Child labourers' perceptions on their own future were very interesting as most child labourers considered their life as very harsh but most of them somewhat accepted their harsh life as their destiny. The author found during this fieldwork that most of these child labourers thought that some change might happen in their life by which they meant they expected that they might earn more for better support of their families in future.

(i) Statistical Analyses on the Marginalisation of Population and Child Labour

The author has also analysed the results of some statistical tests which he had conducted on some of the selected families in the studied populations. The author actually made random selections of 10 families each from Population-I and Population-II (thus making 20 families from the Control Group) and 20 families from Population-III (i.e. the Programme Group) to gauge the differences in marginalisation among these groups of population and its correlation with the phenomenon of child labour. One of these observations was that the households (or their landlords) in the Control Group were deprived of any legitimate rights on the structure in which they were living whereas each of the households (or their landlords) in the Programme Group did have the legitimacy of their housing structure. This difference was clearly reflected as the Control Group of population became more marginalised than the Programme Group of population in the city of Kolkata. Housing condition and some collective consumption facilities necessary for day-to-day living were also identified. The scores were assigned to those according to their level of convenience and quality among the 20 households in the Control Group and 20 households in the Programme

Group to see whether, as far as these parameters on urban marginalisation were concerned, any distinctive features were discernible among these population groups. Statistical tests in this regard showed that the Programme Group population was enjoying significantly better accommodation as far as the condition of housing, the nature of housing, the latrine facility and the access to drinking water facility were concerned. This should lead the rejection of null hypothesis of equality of access to collective consumptions i.e. the government provided basic amenities. On the question of the participation of children in economic activity the author tested 20 households from the Control Group (10 households each from Population-I and Population-II) and 20 households from the Programme Group and found (by chi-square test) that in the Control Group there was much higher propensity of children to enter into the labour market and the tendency was comparatively much lower among children of the Programme Group. Similarly on the question of the participation of children in school among the two groups of populations the author found that the null hypothesis of no association must be rejected as the children of the Programme Group were more keen to go to school than their the Control Group counterparts. Thus a positive correlation could be established between the level of urban marginality and the tendency of school-going among the children. Such a tendency of dropping-out from school had always proved to be conducive towards the proliferation of child labour in a population particularly in the Third World.

TOWARDS A THIRD WORLDLY DISCOURSE

Thus one can conclude that the phenomenon of child labour in the Third World demands a fresh look from the researchers as the existing explanations cannot adequately explain the actual problem particularly the nature and cause of the creation as well as the proliferation of child labour in the Third World. This inadequacy has actually deferred the emergence of the ways of solving or ameliorating the situation. But at the same time funds worth billions of dollars are getting mobilised from the national and international agencies on the existing body of knowledge and analyses on child labour in the Third World.

Most of these analyses have emanated either from the Western observers or originated from the Western views on this problem.

This work showed that the phenomenon of child labour could not be explained in isolation and complete paradigm shift is required in the analyses of this problem. In a traditional society like India most of the child labourers have a family and it is the family which decides on how the time of the child would be allocated in the household work, gainful work, play, leisure, education and other such activities. So one should analyse the child labour problem from the family level as in this study the author found it was that the level of urban marginality of the family that formed an important component for the creation of child labour. Thus when the families slipped below a certain threshold level of marginality parents tended to release their children for work as a part of the survival strategy of those families. Thus in the Control Group in this study, which was living without any security of tenure and was living under constant threat of eviction, the author found that more families released their children for work. In the Programme Group, living with security of tenure and was not under any threat of eviction, very few families were prepared to release their children for work and the parents were investing more on their future i.e. on the education of their children.

In addition, the effects of globalisation on the marginalised families living without any security of tenure of their settlements were getting worse as revealed from this study. These marginal settlements were getting evicted regularly to undertake various city development programmes to attract new capitals since the cities became new destinations of the national and international capitals courtesy the neo-liberal model of world economy. So the problem of child labour can only be analysed properly in the backdrop of various local and global factors which are unique to the individual Third World situations. The author argues that more such ethnographic works on the Third World child labour situation can only explain the problem properly which has become absolutely imperative for the amelioration of this problem in the Third World.

Bibliography

Bagchi, S.S. and A. Das, 2004. "On the Question of Urban Poverty in a Third World Context". *Journal of the Department of Anthropology*. University of Calcutta, Vol. 8-9, Issue 1-2.

Bagchi, S.S., 2009. *Expanding Horizons of Human Rights*. New Delhi: Atlantic Publishers & Distributors (P) Ltd.

Bernard, H.R., 1988. *Research Methods in Cultural Anthropology*. Newbury Park, CA: Sage.

Bourgois, P., 1995. *In Search of Respect: Selling Crack in El Barrio*. New York: Cambridge University Press.

Burra, N., 1987. Report on Child Labour in the Lock Industry of Aligarh, Uttar Pradesh. New Delhi, Prepared for UNICEF.

——, 1989. Child Labour in the Brassware Industries of Moradabad, Uttar Pradesh, India. New Delhi, Prepared for ILO.

Butcher, K.F. and A. Case, 1994. "The Effect of Sibling Sex Composition on Women's Education and Earnings". *The Quarterly Journal of Economics*, Vol. 109 (3). pp. 531-63.

Castells, M., 1977. *The Urban Question: A Marxist Approach*. Translated by Alan Sheridan. London: Edward Arnold (original publication in French, 1972).

——, 1983. *The City and the Grassroots: A Cross-cultural Theory of Urban Social Movements*. Berkeley, CA: University of California Press.

——, 1993. "European Cities, the Informational Society, the Global Economy". In L. Deben, W. Helinemeijer, and D. Van der Vaart (eds.). *Understanding Amsterdam: Essays on Economic Vitality, City Life and Urban Form*. Madrid: Sistena, DI.

Castells, M. and J.H. Mollenkopf, 1991. *Dual City: Restructuring New York (The City in the Twenty-first Century)*. New York: Russell Sage Foundation.

Census of India, 1961. *Housing and Establishment Tables*, Table E-1, New Delhi: RGI, Government of India.

——, 1971. *Housing Tables*, Table IV-B, New Delhi: RGI, Government of India.

——, 1981a. *Housing Tables*, Table H-I, New Delhi: RGI, Government of India.

——, 1981b. *Household Tables*, Table HH-l, New Delhi: RGI, Government of India.

Chandhoke, N., 1999. "A Nation Searching for a Narrative in Times of Globalisation". In *Economic and Political Weekly*. May 1-7.

CMDA (now KMDA), 1981. *Report No. 132*, Calcutta: CMDA.

——, 1982. *Perspectives and Programmes for Shelter in Calcutta Metropolitan District*. Calcutta: CMDA.

Department of Education, MHRD, 1999. *Annual Report 1998–1999*. New Delhi: Department of Education, MHRD, Government of India.

Dingwaney, G., 1988. *Children of Darkness: A Manual on Child Labour in India*. New Delhi: Rural Labour Cell, GOI.

Fyfe, A., 1989. *Child Labour*. Cambridge: Polity Press.

Garg, A. and J. Morduch, 1998. "Sibling Rivalry and the Gender Gap: Evidence from Child Health Outcomes in Ghana". *Journal of Population Economics*, Vol. 11 (4). pp. 471-93. December.

Government of India, "National Commission on Urbanisation, 1988". *Report*, Vol. II. New Delhi: Government of India.

——, 1991. Instruction to enumerators for filling up the household schedule and individual slip. Office of the Registrar General and Census Commissioner for India,

Ministry of Home Affairs, New Delhi: Government of India.

Government of India, Ministry of Health, 1988. *Health Information, India*, New Delhi: Government of India.

Greene, J.C., V.J. Caracelli and W.F. Graham, 1989. "Toward a Conceptual Framework for Mixed-Method Evaluation Design." *Educational Evaluation and Policy Analysis*, 11(3), pp. 255-74.

ILO (International Labour Office), 1998. *Child Labour: Targeting the Intolerable.* Geneva: International Labour Organization.

——, 2001. *World Employment Report 2001.* Geneva: International Labour Organization.

Institute of Applied Manpower Research, 1995. *Status and Problems of Leather Workers and their Future Growth Perspective: A Study Based on Survey on Leather Workers in Unorganized Sector in the Districts of Agra.* New Delhi: Institute of Applied Manpower Research.

Jensen, R.T., 1999. "Patterns, Causes and Consequences of Child Labour in Pakistan," mimeo, John F. Kennedy School of Government, Harvard University, June.

——, 2000. "Agricultural Volatility and Investments in Children". *American Economic Review*, May, 90(2): pp. 399-404.

Jhabvala, R., R. Dhawan, K. Mahajan, 1991. *Women Who Roll Bidis: Two Studies of Gujarat.* New Delhi: Kalpaz.

Karunanidhi, G., 1995. *A Study on the Beedi Workers of North Arcot District.* New Delhi: ICSSR.

Kothari, R. (ed.), 1970. *Caste in Indian Politics.* New Delhi: Orient Longmans.

Kumar, B. and G. Biswas, 1992. *A Study of Problems of Working Children in Lock-making Industry, Aligarh, (U.P.)*, Allahabad. New Delhi: Manohar.

——, 1992. *A Study of Problems of Working Children in Brassware Industry of Moradabad (U.P.).* Allahabad. New Delhi: Manohar.

Liebow, E., 1967. *Tally's Corner: A Study of Negro Street Corner Men*. Boston: Rowman and Littlefield.

Lieten, G.K. and B. White, 2001. *Child Labour Policy Options*. Amsterdam: Aksant.

Majumdar, B., 2001. "ILO Slams India for Child Labour Cover-up". *The Statesman*, May, 28.

Menon, S., 1979. "Sivakasi: The 'Little Japan' of India". *The Times of India*. October 7.

Naidu, R., et. al., 1992. *Child Labour in Slate Mines and Factories of Markapur, Andhra Pradesh*, New Delhi: Vikas.

Nangia, S., 1988. *Carpet Weaving Industries in Jammu and Kashmir*. UNICEF Regional Office for South-Central Asia. New Delhi: UNICEF.

National Institute of Urban Affairs, 1988. *Who the Poor Are? What they Do? Where they Live?* New Delhi: National Institute of Urban Affairs.

National Sample Survey Organisation (NSSO), 1987a. *Table with Notes on Particulars of Dwelling Units*, NSS, 38th Round, Department of Statistics, Ministry of Planning and Programme Implementation, New Delhi: NSSO.

——, 1987b. *Tables with Notes on Particulars of Dwelling Units,* Thirty-eighth Round (Jan-Dec. 1983), Number 339. New Delhi: NSSO.

——, 1989. *Morbidity and Utilisation of Medical Services*, NSS, 42nd Round, Department of Statistics, Ministry of Planning and Programme Implementation, New Delhi: NSSO.

——, 1990. "A Profile of Households and Population by Economic Class and Social Group and Availability of Drinking Water, Electricity and Disinfection of Dwelling". 42nd Round, *Sarvekshana*, 13(4), Government of India, New Delhi: NSSO.

——, 1997a. Slums in India, NSS 49th Round, Department of Statistics, Ministry of Planning and Programme Implementation, New Delhi: NSSO.

——, 1997b. *Dwellings in India*. NSS 50th Round, Department of Statistics, Ministry of Planning and Programme Implementation, New Delhi: NSSO.

——, 1998a. Housing Conditions in India, NSS 49th Round, Department of Statistics, Ministry of Planning and Programme Implementation, New Delhi: NSSO.

——, 1998b. *The Aged in India: A Socio-Economic Profile*. Department of Statistics, Ministry of Planning and Programme Implementation, New Delhi: NSSO.

——, 1998c. "Attending an Educational Institution in India: It's Level, Nature and Cost", NSS 52nd Round, July 1995-June 1996, Report No. 439; Department of Statistics, Government of India, New Delhi: NSSO.

——, 1998d. 1997—NSSO 53rd Round as reported in *Selected Educational Statistics; 1998-99*. Department of Education, MHRD Table 13, New Delhi: NSSO.

——, 2001. *Employment and Unemployment Situation in India—1999-2000, Part I, NSS 55th Round (July 1999-June 2000), Report No. 458*; Ministry of Statistics and Programme Implementation, New Delhi: NSSO.

NCAER, 1999a. "Micro Impacts of Macroeconomic and Adjustment Policies" (MIMAP)—*India*, October, Volume 1, Issue 1.

——, 1999b. *India Human Development Report of the Nineties*. New Delhi: NCAER.

Pande, P.N. and G.P. Mishra, 1996. *Child Labour in the Glass Industry*. New Delhi: Nangia.

Pritchett, L.H., 1994. "Desired Fertility and the Impact of Population Policies". *Population & Development Review*, Vol. 20 (1). pp. 1-55. March.

Raja, D.V.P., 1993. *Research Study on Child Labour in Match Industries in Sivakasi*. Madurai: Madurai Institute of Social Work.

Raman, V., 1998. Globalization and Child Labour. *Revolutionary Democracy*, Vol. IV, No. 1, April.

Registrar General of India. "Provisional Population Totals: Workers and Non-workers". *Census of India, 1981*. Paper 3, Series 1. New Delhi: RGI.

——, 1996. "Social and Cultural Table". *Census of India 1991, Part IV*. New Delhi: RGI.

——, 1997a. "Age, Sex and Educational Level, Table C-2". *Census of India 1991*. New Delhi: RGI.

——, 1999a. "Compendium of India's Fertility and Mortality Indicators 1971 to 1997". Based on Sample Registration System. New Delhi: RGI.

——, 1999b. *Ageing Population of India: An Analysis of the 1991 Census Data*. New Delhi: RGI.

——, 2001. "Provisional Population Totals", Paper 1, 2001, Statement 19. New Delhi: RGI.

Sharma, A.N., R. Sharma and N. Raj, 2000. "The Impact of Social Labelling on Child Labour in India's Carpet Industry". ILO/IPEC Working Paper. New Delhi: Institute for Human Development.

Singh, G., 1982. "At Sivakasi", *The Economic Times*, April 10.

Singh, J., 1984. "Torture Camp of Mirzapur". *The Times of India*, April 11.

Singh, M., V.D. Kaura and S.A. Khan, 1980. *Working Children in Bombay—A Study*. New Delhi: National Institute of Public Cooperation and Child Development.

Singer, M., 1955. "The Cultural Pattern of Indian Civilization". In *The Far Eastern Quarterly*, Vol. 15, No. 1.

——, 1958. *Traditional India: Structure and Change*. JAF: Vol. 78, No. 281.

——, 1972. *When a Great Tradition Modernizes: An Anthropological Approach to Indian Civilization*. New York: Praeger Publishers.

UNDP (United Nations Development Programme), 1990. *Human Development Report, 1990*. New York: UNDP.

——, 1995. *Human Development Report, 1995*. Oxford: UNDP.

——, 1998a. *Human Development Report, 1998*. New York: UNDP.

——, 1998b. *Overcoming Human Poverty: UNDP Poverty Report, 1998*. New York: UNDP.

UNICEF (United Nations Children's Fund), 2002. *The State of the World's Children, 2002*. New York: UNICEF.

United Nations, 1990. *World Urbanization Prospects, 1990*. New York: United Nations.

——, 1995. *Programme of Action of the World Summit for Social Development*. New York: United Nations.

——, 1996a. *The Right to Adequate Housing*. Prepared by Rajindar Sachar, Special Rapporteur of the Sub-Committee on Prevention of Discrimination and Protection of Minorities, Centre for Human Rights, Geneva: United Nations, 1996b. *World Urbanization Prospects: The 1996 Revision*. New York: United Nations.

——, 1998. *Principles and Recommendation for Population and Housing Censuses*. Statistical Papers, Series M No. 67/ Rev. 1. Sales No. E.98.XVII. 8, New York: United Nations.

Venkatramani, S.H., 1983. 'Tamil Nadu: Vested Interests', *India Today*, July 15.

Vijaygopalan, S., 1993. *Child Labour in Carpet Industry: A Status Report*. Working Paper. National Council of Applied Economic Research, New Delhi.

Appendix

PLATES

Plate A1: The Picture from the Field (The Settlement)

Plate A2: The Picture from the Field (The Settlement Beside the Railway Tract)

Plate A3: The Picture from the Field (The Waste/Rag Pickers)

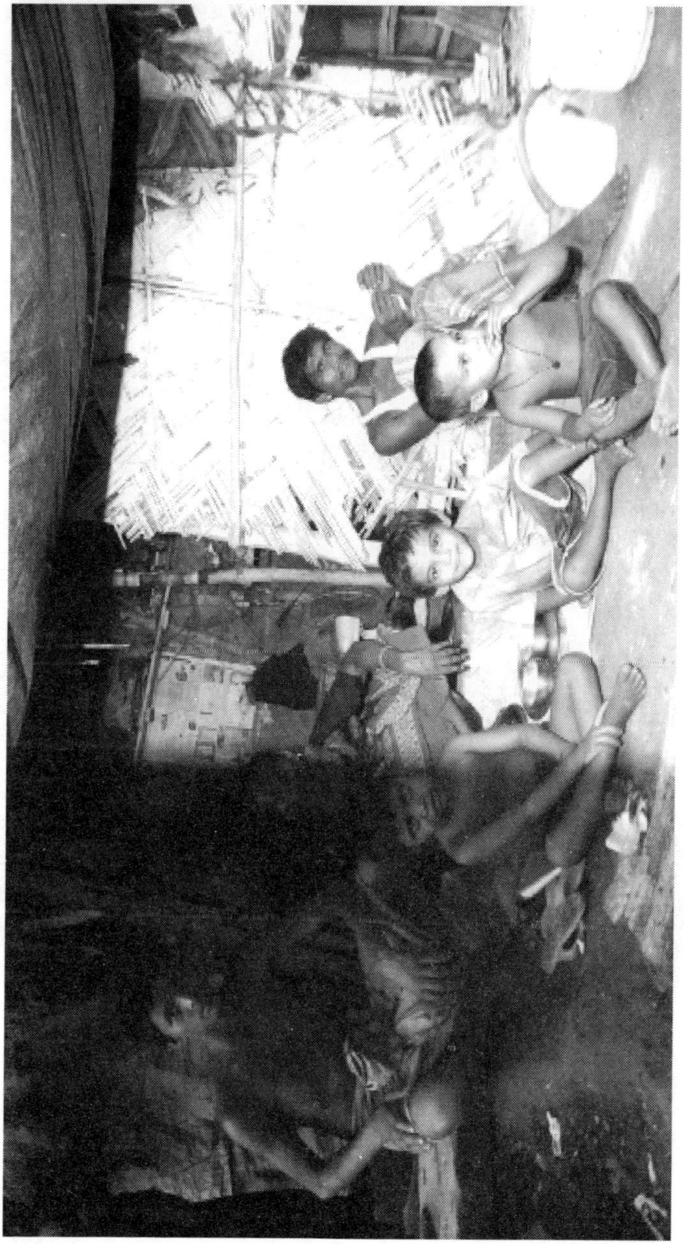

Plate A4: The Picture from the Field (A Family of Child Labourers)

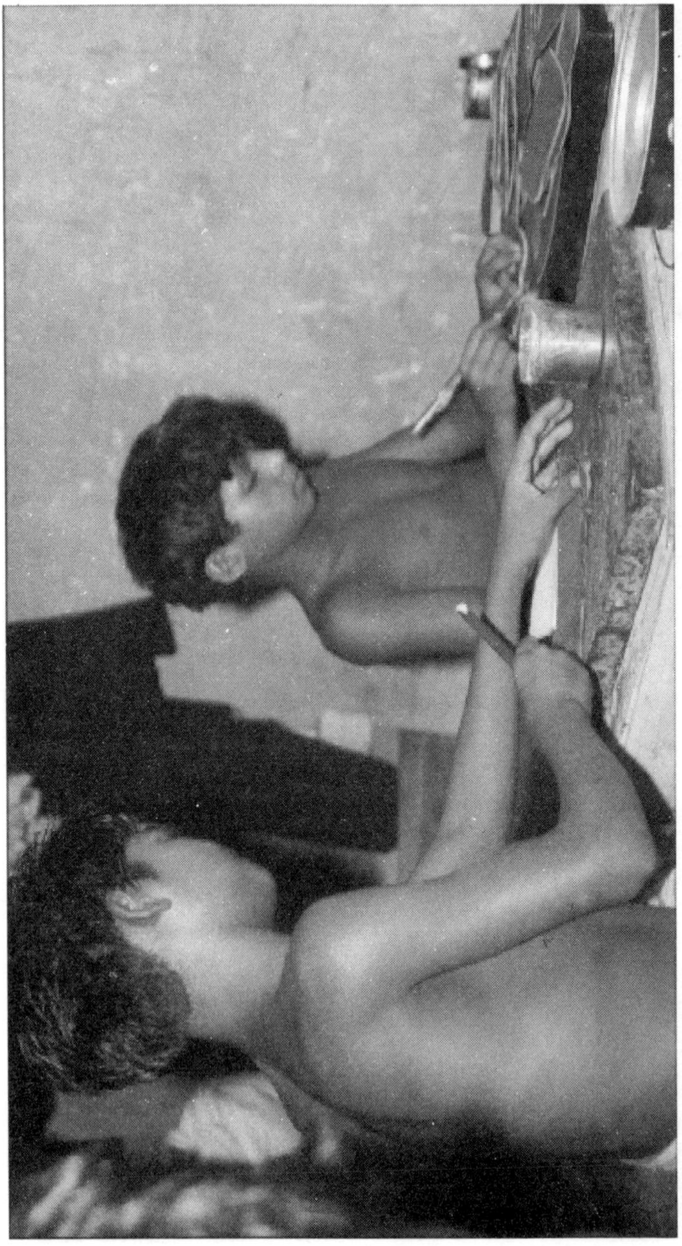

Plate A5: The Picture from the Field (Children Working in a Small Workshop)

Index

Bagchi, S.S., 2
Biswas, G., 10
Bourgois, P., 133
Bernard, R., 35
Burra, N., 10
Butcher, K.F., 32

Calcutta Thika and Other Tenancies and Land (Acquisition and Regulation) Act, 1981, 3, 34, 38, 93, 133
Case, A., 32
Castells, M., 2
child labour:
    determinants of, 5-7
    constitutional safeguards, 13-14
    legal provisions India,
        before independence, 14-15
        after independence, 15-19
    magnitude of the problem of, 7-9
    national initiatives on, 10-21
    international initiatives on, 21-29
    official reports on child labour in India, 10-13
    social labelling, 27-29
    supreme court judgment on, 18-19
Convention on the Rights of the Child (CRC), 21

Deaton, A., 25-26, 32
Dingwaney, G., 9

field methods:
    data analysis, 37
    free lists and ranking, 37, 134
    gaining entry, 35, 133
    non-participant observation, 36-37, 133
    participant observation, 37, 133
    rapport building, 35-36, 133
    selecting a key informant, 36, 133
    selection of informants, 36, 133
    site selection, 34-35, 133
Fyfe, A., 5

Garg, A., 32
GATT, 1
Giri Institute of Development Studies, 10

ILO, 5, 8, 21-27, 29-31
ILO Conventions, 21-25
Indian Institute of Health Management Research, 10
Institute of Applied Manpower Research, 10
International Labour Standards, 22-23
International Programme on the Elimination of the Child Labour (IPEC), 26-27

Jensen, R., 32
Jhabvala, R., 10

Kanjibhai Desai Samaj Shikshan Bhavan Trust, 10
Karunanidhi, G., 10
Kothari, R., 9
Kruijtbosch, M., 9-10
Kumar, B., 10

learning without frontiers, 29
Liebow, E., 133

major child labour intensive occupation in India, 9-10
Majumdar, B., 8
Menon, S., 9
Morduch, J., 32

Naidu, R., 9
Nangia, S., 10
National Labour Institute, 10
national child labour policy, 19-20
national child labour projects (NCLP), 20

Operation Research Group (ORG), 9-10

Pande, P.N., 10
programme for street children, 29

Raja, D.V.P., 9
Raman, V., 10

Structural Adjustment Programmes (SAP), 1-2, 130
Singh, J., 9
Singh, G., 10
South Asia Poverty Alleviation Programme, 29

UNAIDS, 21, 29
UNDP, 21, 29
UNDCP, 21, 29
UNICEF, 21, 29
UNFPA, 21, 29
UNIFEM, 21, 29
UNESCO, 21, 29
urban marginalisation, 92, 133, 135-46

Vijaygopalan, S., 10
Vinkatramani, S.H., 9

WTO, 1, 130